# PROJECT
# SUCCESS 3

Nancy Blodgett Matsunaga
Sheena M. Macpherson

*Series Consultants*
Susan Gaer
Sarah Lynn

*The publisher would like to thank Irene Frankel for her creative conception and vision for this groundbreaking course.*

**PROJECT SUCCESS** 3

Pearson Education, 10 Bank Street, White Plains, NY 10606

**Staff Credits:** The people who made up the *Project Success* team, representing editorial, production, design, and manufacturing, are Peter Benson, Andrea Bryant, Maretta Callahan, Iris Candelaria, Aerin Csigay, Mindy DePalma, Dave Dickey, Christine Edmonds, Nancy Flaggman, Ann France, Aliza Greenblatt, Gosia Jaros-White, Caroline Kasterine, Amy Kefauver, Niki Lee, Jaime Lieber, Jessica Miller-Smith, Tracey Munz Cataldo, Laurie Neaman, Jenn Raspiller, Julie Schmidt, Kim Snyder, Katherine Sullivan, Loretta Steeves, Jane Townsend, Ken Volcjak, and Martin Yu.

**Interior Design:** Word & Image

**Cover Design:** Ann France and Tracey Munz Cataldo

**Text Composition:** TSI Graphics

**Text font:** Franklin Gothic

For photo and illustration credits, please turn to the back of the book.

**Library of Congress Cataloging-in-Publication Data**
Lynn, Sarah.
  Project success : skills for the 21st century / Sarah Lynn ; Series Consultants: Susan Gaer, Sarah Lynn.
       pages cm
  Summary: Project Success is a blended-learning digital and print course with a strong focus on workplace skills, career readiness, and 21st century challenges. This unique video-based series engages learners with high-interest video vignettes that represent a "day in the life" of characters in diverse workplace settings that may simulate their own. Integrated skills lessons encourage critical thinking and problem solving woven into the students' English language learning journey.
  ISBN 978-0-13-294236-2 — ISBN 978-0-13-248297-4 — ISBN 978-0-13-294238-6 — ISBN 978-0-13-294240-9 — ISBN 978-0-13-294242-3 — ISBN 978-0-13-298513-0
  1. English language—Textbooks for foreign speakers. 2. English language—Spoken English. 3. English language—Sound recordings for foreign speakers. 4. English language—Study and teaching—Foreign speakers—Audio-visual aids. 5. Business communication—United States—Vocational guidance. I. Gaer, Susan. II. Title.
  PE1128.L98 2014
  428.2'4—dc23
                                                                            2013035851

ISBN-10: 0-13-294240-2
ISBN-13: 978-0-13-294240-9

Printed in the United States of America
4   17

# Contents

Acknowledgments ................................................. iv

About the Series Consultants and Authors ........................ v

Scope and Sequence.............................................. vi–ix

To the Teacher.................................................. x

To the Student ................................................. 1


**WELCOME UNIT** ................................................ 2

**UNIT 1 Frank's Short Day** ................................... 5

**UNIT 2 Biata's Crazy Day**................................... 19

**UNIT 3 Susan's Cares and Concerns** ......................... 33

**UNIT 4 Henry's Big Dreams** ................................. 47

**UNIT 5 Alina on the Move**................................... 61

**UNIT 6 Biata Helps Out** .................................... 75

**UNIT 7 Frank Makes Time** ................................... 89

**UNIT 8 Susan at Work and Play** ............................. 103

**UNIT 9 Alina Returns** ...................................... 117

**UNIT 10 Henry Takes Steps**................................. 131


Grammar Review ................................................ 145

Grammar References............................................. 161

Word List ..................................................... 162

# Acknowledgments

The authors and publisher would like to offer sincere thanks to our Series Consultants for lending their expertise and insights and for helping shape the course.

**Susan Gaer** Santa Ana College School of Continuing Education, Santa Ana, CA

**Sarah Lynn** Harvard Bridge to Learning and Literacy Program, Cambridge, MA

In addition, we would like to express gratitude to the following people. Their kind participation was invaluable to the creation of this program.

*Consultants*

**Robert Breitbard**, Director of Adult & Community Education, Collier County Public Schools, Naples, Florida; **Ingrid Greenberg**, Associate Professor, ESL, and Past-President, Academic Senate, Continuing Education, San Diego Community College District, San Diego, California; **Vittoria G. Maghsoudi-Abbate**, Assistant Director, Mt. Diablo Adult Education, Mt. Diablo USD, Concord, California; **Irina Patten**, Lone Star College-Fairbanks Center, Houston, Texas; **Maria Soto Caratini**, Eastfield College DCCCD, Mesquite, Texas; **Claire Valier**, Palm Beach County, Florida; **Jacqueline S. Walpole**, Director, Adult Education, Prince George's Community College, Largo, Maryland.

*Reviewers*

**Eleanor Brockman-Forfang**, Instructor, Special Projects (ESL), Tarrant County College, South Campus, Fort Worth, TX; **Natalya Dollar**, ESL Program Resource Coordinator, North Orange County Community College District, Anaheim, CA; **Bette Empol**, ESL, ABE, GED Prep and Bridge Coordinator, Conejo Valley Adult School, Thousand Oaks, CA; **Mark Fisher**, Lone Star College-Fairbanks Center, Houston, TX; **Ann Fontanella**, ESL Instructor, City College of San Francisco, San Francisco, CA; **Ingrid Greenberg**, Associate Professor, ESL, and Past-President, Academic Senate, Continuing Education, San Diego Community College District, San Diego, CA; **Janet Harclerode**, Santa Monica College, Santa Monica, CA; **Laura Jensen**, ESL Instructor, North Seattle Community College, Seattle, WA; **Tommie Martinez**, Fresno Adult School, Fresno, CA; **Suzanne L. Monti**, ESOL Instructional Specialist, Community College of Baltimore County, Continuing Education, Baltimore, MD; **Kelly Nusz**, Carlos Rosario Charter School, Washington, D.C; **Irina Patten**, Lone Star College-Fairbanks Center, Houston, TX; **Ariel Peckokas**, Collier County Public Schools Adult Education, Naples, FL; **Sydney Rice**, Imperial Valley College, Imperial, CA; **Richard Salvador**, McKinley Community Schools of Arts, Honolulu, Hawaii; **Maria Soto Caratini**, Eastfield College DCCCD, Mesquite, TX; **Patty Swartzbaugh**, Nashville Adult Literacy Council, Nashville, TN; **Candace Thompson-Lynch**, ESL Instructor, School of Continuing Education, North Orange County Community College District, Anaheim, CA; **Esther M. Tillet**, Miami Dade College-Wolfson Campus, Miami, FL; **Adriana Treadway**, Assistant Director, Spring International Language Center, University of Arkansas, Fayetteville, AR; **Monica C. Vazquez**, ESOL Adjunct Instructor, Brookhaven College, DCCCD, Farmers Branch, TX.

Thanks also to the teachers who contributed their valuable ideas for the Persistence Activities: **Dave Coleman**, Los Angeles Unified School District, Los Angeles, CA; **Renee Collins**, Elk Grove Adult and Community Education, Elk Grove, CA; **Elaine Klapman**, Venice Community Adult School, Venice, CA (retired); **Yvonne Wong Nishio**, Evans Community Adult School, Los Angeles, CA; **Daniel S. Pittaway**, North Orange County Community College District, Anaheim, CA; **Laurel Pollard**, Educational Consultant, Tucson, AZ; **Eden Quimzon**, Santiago Canyon College, Division of Continuing Education, Orange, CA.

Special thanks also to **Sharon Goldstein** for her skilled writing of the pronunciation strand.

## SERIES CONSULTANTS

**Susan Gaer** has worked as an ESL teacher since 1980 and currently teaches at the Santa Ana College School of Continuing Education. She is an avid user of technology and trains teachers online for TESOL and the Outreach Technical Assistance Center (OTAN). Susan is a frequent presenter at local, state, national, and international conferences on using the latest technology with adult learners from the literacy level through transition to college. She has co-authored books and teacher manuals, served on the executive boards for CATESOL (California Teachers of English to Speakers of Other Languages) and TESOL, and contributed to standing committees for professional development and technology. Susan holds a master's degree in English with emphasis in TESOL from San Francisco State University and a master's degree in Educational Technology from Pepperdine University.

**Sarah Lynn** has over twenty-five years of teaching experience in ESOL. She has dedicated much of her teaching life to working with low-level learners with interrupted education. Currently she teaches at the Harvard Bridge Program, Harvard University. As a teacher trainer, Sarah has led professional development workshops throughout the United States on topics such as teaching in the multilevel classroom, learner persistence, twenty-first-century skills, self-directed learning, collaborative learning, and scaffolding learning for the literacy learner. As a consultant, she has written ESOL curricula for programs in civics, literacy, phonics, and English language arts. As a materials writer, she has contributed to numerous Pearson ELT publications, including *Business Across Cultures, Future, Future U.S. Citizens*, and *Project Success*. Sarah holds a master's degree in TESOL from Teacher's College, Columbia University.

## AUTHORS

**Nancy Blodgett Matsunaga** has a master's degree in TESOL from Saint Michael's College. She has taught EFL and ESL classes in Japan, Colombia, and various programs in the United States. She worked for eight years as a development editor and project manager with Pearson, where she focused on multimedia, assessment, and adult education titles, including, among others, *Longman English Online, Worldview, Focus on Grammar, Top Notch*, and *Future: English for Success*. She currently lives with her family in Munich, Germany, where she teaches creative writing courses to native and non-native English speakers.

**Sheena M. Macpherson** has worked in the ESL field for more than 20 years as a teacher and as a program administrator. She has a master's degree in TESOL from Saint Michael's College, where she taught students in both the Intensive English Program and the Academic English Bridge Program. She served as Director of those programs for several years. Additionally, she has been a teacher trainer both in the United States and overseas in areas of curriculum, CALL, and practicum. Recently she has been working with refugees in the Vermont Refugee Resettlement Program.

# Scope and Sequence 3

| Unit | Listening/Speaking VIDEO | Grammar VIDEO | Practical Skills | Pronunciation | Reading Skills |
|---|---|---|---|---|---|
| **Welcome** page 2 | • Meet your classmates<br>• Talk about your goals<br>• Ask for and give clarification | | | | |
| **1** **Frank's Short Day** page 5 | • Make small talk<br>• Ask to leave work early<br>• Ask to borrow something | • Adverbs of frequency: *always, usually, often, sometimes, rarely, never*<br>• Quantifiers: *a few, many, all, a lot, most, some, none* | • Read prescription and OTC medicine labels | • Intonation in sentences with direct address<br>• Sentence rhythm: stressed and unstressed words | • Make predictions<br>an article about the importance of a nutritious breakfast |
| **2** **Biata's Crazy Day** page 19 | • Call in late to work<br>• Ask for help at work<br>• Give driving directions | • Future Forms: *be going to, will*, present continuous with future meaning<br>• Past ability with *be able to* and *could* | • Read a street map | • Weak pronunciation of pronouns and contractions with *be* and *will*<br>• The vowel sounds /eɪ/ (save) and /ɛ/ (well) | • Skim for the general idea<br>a blog post with strange reasons people give for being late |
| **3** **Susan's Cares and Concerns** page 33 | • Talk about things you used to do<br>• Report an accident at work<br>• Ask for and give clarification | • *Used to* for habitual past actions<br>• Past continuous | • Talk about workplace safety | • Relaxed pronunciation of *used to*<br>• Word stress: highlighting the most important word | • Scan for details<br>An article about community responses to distracted driving |
| **4** **Henry's Big Dreams** page 47 | • Talk about a job you want<br>• Talk about your work history<br>• Offer to help someone | • Present perfect: indefinite past<br>• Present perfect: *for/ since* | • Read a pay stub | • Pronouncing abbreviations<br>• Silent letters | • Use supporting illustrations and examples<br>an article about unusual jobs |
| **5** **Alina on the Move** page 61 | • Talk about exercise habits<br>• Ask for and give advice<br>• Ask about an apartment for rent | • Gerunds and infinitives<br>• Gerunds after prepositions | • Read an apartment rental ad | • Weak pronunciation of *do you* ("d'ya")<br>• Stressed syllables in words | • Recognize antecedents<br>a message board offering advice about workplace problems |

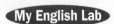

| | | | |
|---|---|---|---|
| Vocabulary | Practical Skills | Writing | Unit Tests |
| Listening and Speaking | Grammar | Job-Seeking | Midterm Tests |
| Pronunciation | Reading | | Final CASAS Test Prep |

| Writing Skills | Vocabulary Skills | Job-Seeking Skills | Career Pathways | CASAS Highlights | Common Core College and Career Readiness |
|---|---|---|---|---|---|
| | | | | 0.1.1, 0.1.2, 0.1.4, 0.1.5, 0.1.6, 7.1.1, 7.4.6 | |
| • Describe a workplace problem<br>• Give examples | • Identify synonyms<br>Learning strategy: Draw pictures<br>Word list page 162 | • Assess your work needs | • Develop interpersonal relationships<br>• Communicate ideas clearly<br>• Be self-aware | 0.1.2, 0.1.4, 0.2.4, 1.6.1, 3.3.1, 3.3.2, 3.4.1, 3.4.2, 3.5.1, 3.5.2, 4.1.9, 4.2.5, 4.6.2, 6.6.5, 6.7.4, 7.2.4, 7.2.5, 7.3.1, 7.3.2, 7.4.2, 7.4.3, 7.4.4, 7.4.8, 7.5.5 | R.1, 2, 4, 5, 7, 10<br>W.1, 2, 4, 5, 7<br>SL.1, 2, 3, 4<br>L.1, 2, 4, 5, 6 |
| • Give instructions<br>• Use transitional phrases (first of all, then, finally) | • Identify antonyms<br>Learning strategy: Group by meanings<br>Word list page 162 | • Assess your job skills | • Deal with difficult situations<br>• Ask for help<br>• Delegate responsibility<br>• Be self-aware | 0.1.2, 0.1.4, 0.1.7, 2.2.1, 2.2.5, 4.1.9, 4.4.1, 4.4.2, 4.5.7, 4.6.2, 4.8.2, 6.7.4, 7.2.3, 7.2.5, 7.4.2, 7.4.3, 7.4.4, 7.4.8, 7.5.1 | R.1, 2, 4, 5, 7, 10<br>W.2, 4, 5, 7<br>SL.1, 2, 3, 4<br>L.1, 2, 4, 5, 6 |
| • Write a letter of opinion<br>• Use transition words (also, therefore, however) | • Understand prefixes<br>Learning strategy: Learn words that go together<br>Word list page 163 | • Read job ads | • Manage emotions<br>• Offer solutions to problems<br>• Ask for clarification | 0.1.2, 0.1.3, 0.1.4, 0.1.6, 0.2.4, 3.1.3, 3.4.2, 3.6.4, 4.1.3, 4.3.1, 4.3.2, 4.3.4, 4.4.1, 6.7.2, 7.2.5, 7.2.6, 7.2.7, 7.3.1, 7.3.2, 7.4.2, 7.4.3, 7.4.4 | R.1, 3, 4, 7, 10<br>W.1, 2, 4, 5, 7<br>SL.1, 2, 4<br>L.1, 2, 4, 5, 6 |
| • Write a short biography<br>• Focus on one main idea in each paragraph | • Understand suffixes<br>Learning strategy: Write in your first language<br>Word list page 163 | • Read and complete a job application Part 1: Personal information | • Network<br>• Ask questions<br>• Help others | 0.1.2, 0.1.6, 0.1.8, 4.1.2, 4.1.8, 4.1.9, 4.2.1, 4.4.7, 4.6.3, 4.7.3, 6.6.5, 6.7.2, 7.2.5, 7.4.2, 7.4.3, 7.4.4, 7.4.8, 7.5.4 | R.1, 2, 4, 5, 7, 10<br>W.2, 3, 4, 5, 7<br>SL.1, 2, 4<br>L.1, 2, 4, 5, 6 |
| • Write about cause and effect<br>• Use transition words (since, because, as a result) | • Recognize similes<br>Learning strategy: Make word webs<br>Word list page 164 | • Read and complete a job application Part 2: Work history | • Develop interpersonal relationships<br>• Deal with difficult personalities<br>• Navigate office politics<br>• Mentor others<br>• Promote yourself | 0.1.2, 0.1.3, 0.2.4, 1.4.1, 1.4.2, 3.5.1, 3.5.9, 3.6.3, 4.1.2, 4.4.3, 7.2.2, 7.2.3, 7.2.5, 7.2.6, 7.2.8, 7.3.1, 7.3.2, 7.4.2, 7.4.3, 7.4.4, 7.4.8 | R.1, 2, 4, 5, 7, 8, 10<br>W.2, 4, 5, 7<br>SL.1, 2, 3, 4<br>L.1, 2, 4, 5, 6 |

For complete correlations please visit www.pearsoneltusa.com/projectsuccess

# Scope and Sequence 3

| Unit | Listening/Speaking **VIDEO** | Grammar **VIDEO** | Practical Skills | Pronunciation | Reading Skills |
|---|---|---|---|---|---|
| **6** <br> **Biata Helps Out** <br> page 75 | • Assign tasks at work <br> • Take phone messages <br> • Call to change an appointment | • Requests with *can, will, could, would, would you mind* <br> • Indirect objects | • Complete a medical history form | • Weak pronunciation and linking of object pronouns <br> • The reduced vowel /ə/ in unstressed syllables and words | • Make inferences <br> an article offering tips on how to communicate with a health care provider |
| **7** <br> **Frank Makes Time** <br> page 89 | • Give multi-step instructions <br> • Give a progress report at work <br> • Ask to change shifts with someone | • Adverb clauses of time: *when, before, after, as* <br> • Present perfect with *already* and *yet* | • Read a work schedule | • Intonation in complex sentences <br> • The consonant sounds /ʃ/ (<u>she</u>) and /tʃ/ (<u>check</u>) | • Determine the author's purpose <br> an interview with a volunteer at a school reading program |
| **8** <br> **Susan at Work and Play** <br> page 103 | • Get a performance evaluation at work <br> • Ask about someone's belongings <br> • Talk about personal interests | • Present perfect continuous <br> • Possessive pronouns | • Complete a credit card application | • Pronunciation of *I'd like* and *I like* <br> • Pronunciation of *-s* endings | • Identify cause and effect relationships <br> an article offering advice on choosing a credit card |
| **9** <br> **Alina Returns** <br> page 117 | • Talk about how to get a good deal <br> • Compare ways of buying things <br> • Talk about holiday plans | • Present real conditional <br> • Comparatives with *-er, more, less* | • Read a store policy for merchandise returns | • Stress in compound nouns <br> • Two pronunciations of *the* and *to* | • Interpret signal words (*first, before, such as*) <br> an article featuring tips for saving money at the supermarket |
| **10** <br> **Henry Takes Steps** <br> page 131 | • Talk about getting ahead on the job <br> • Talk about someone you admire <br> • Talk about long-term goals | • Future real conditionals <br> • Superlatives with *-est, most, least* | • Read a college course catalog | • Stress in long words <br> • Consonant clusters | • Distinguish between facts and opinions <br> an editorial column debating the value of a college education |

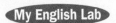

**My English Lab**

| | | | |
|---|---|---|---|
| Vocabulary | Practical Skills | Writing | Unit Tests |
| Listening and Speaking | Grammar | Job-Seeking | Midterm Tests |
| Pronunciation | Reading | | Final CASAS Test Prep |

| Writing Skills | Vocabulary Skills | Job-Seeking Skills | Career Pathways | CASAS Highlights | Common Core College and Career Readiness |
|---|---|---|---|---|---|
| • Write a narrative paragraph<br>• Use phrases of time and place (*in the morning, back at home*) | • Identify collocations<br>Learning strategy: Group words by number of syllables<br>Word list page 164 | • Find job-seeking resources at the library | • Show leadership<br>• Delegate responsibility<br>• Prioritize tasks<br>• Communicate information clearly | 0.1.2, 0.1.6, 0.1.7, 0.2.3, 2.1.7, 2.1.8, 2.5.6, 3.1.2, 3.2.1, 3.6.2, 3.6.4, 4.1.3, 4.1.4, 4.5.1, 4.6.1, 4.7.2, 4.7.3, 7.2.3, 7.2.4, 7.2.7, 7.4.2, 7.4.3, 7.4.4, 7.4.8 | R.1, 2, 3, 6, 7, 8, 10<br>W.3, 4, 5, 7<br>SL.1, 2, 4<br>L.1, 2, 4, 6 |
| • Write a descriptive email<br>• Use descriptive adjectives | • Understand word roots<br>Learning strategy: Group words by part of speech<br>Word list page 165 | • Answer common job interview questions | • Mentor others<br>• Show leadership<br>• Ask questions<br>• Report your progress | 0.1.2, 0.1.6, 0.1.7, 0.2.3, 4.1.5, 4.2.4, 4.4.1, 4.4.3, 4.6.1, 4.6.3, 4.6.4, 4.7.3, 4.8.1, 4.8.2, 5.6.2, 5.6.5, 6.7.4, 7.2.3, 7.2.5, 7.4.2, 7.4.3, 7.4.4, 7.4.8 | R.1, 2, 6, 7, 10<br>W.3, 4, 5, 7<br>SL.1, 2, 4<br>L.1, 2, 4, 6 |
| • Write about your goals<br>• Use quantifiable language including numbers, dates, and times | • Identify adverbs<br>Learning strategy: Write personal sentences<br>Word list page 165 | • Ask questions at a job interview | • Accept criticism<br>• Learn from mistakes<br>• Be self-aware<br>• Develop interpersonal relationships | 0.1.2, 0.1.6, 0.2.4, 1.2.1, 1.2.2, 1.2.5, 1.3.2, 1.8.6, 3.5.8, 3.5.9, 4.1.5, 4.4.4, 4.4.5, 5.7.6, 7.2.2, 7.2.5, 7.2.7, 7.4.2, 7.4.3, 7.4.4, 7.5.1 | R.1, 2, 3, 10<br>W.2, 4, 5, 7<br>SL.1, 2, 4<br>L.1, 2, 4, 6 |
| • Write a letter of complaint<br>• Use a business letter format | • Look for context clues<br>Learning strategy: Group by function<br>Word list page 166 | • Recognize illegal job interview questions | • Develop interpersonal relationships<br>• Communicate a complaint<br>• Show tact | 0.1.2, 0.2.4, 1.2.6, 1.3.1, 1.3.3, 1.6.3, 1.6.5, 2.7.1, 2.7.3, 4.1.5, 4.2.6, 4.6.2, 5.7.6, 7.2.3, 7.2.5, 7.4.2, 7.4.3, 7.4.4 | R.1, 2, 4, 10<br>W.4, 5, 7<br>SL.1, 2, 4<br>L.1, 2, 4, 5, 6 |
| • Write a personal narrative about important life events<br>• Use adverbial clauses of time (*After I graduated*) | • Recognize word families<br>Learning strategy: Write a short story<br>Word list page 166 | • Respond to a job offer | • Show persistence<br>• Manage stress<br>• Think on your feet<br>• Network<br>• Make informed decisions | 0.1.2, 0.1.3, 0.2.3, 2.8.1, 2.8.3, 2.8.6, 4.1.4, 4.1.9, 4.2.1, 4.2.5, 4.4.1, 4.4.2, 4.4.5, 6.7.2, 7.1.1, 7.1.2, 7.2.3, 7.2.4, 7.2.5, 7.4.2, 7.4.3, 7.4.4, 7.4.8, 7.6.3 | R.1, 2, 3, 6, 7, 8, 9, 10<br>W.3, 4, 5, 7<br>SL.1, 2, 3, 4<br>L.1, 2, 4, 6 |

# To the Teacher

*Project Success* is a dynamic six-level, four-skills multimedia course for adults and young adults. It offers a comprehensive and integrated program for false-beginner to low-advanced learners, with a classroom and online curriculum correlated to national and state standards.

## KEY FEATURES

In developing this course we focused on our students' future aspirations, and on their current realities. Through inspiring stories of adults working and mastering life's challenges, we illustrate the skills and competencies adult English language learners need to participate fully and progress in their roles at home, work, school, and in the community. To create versatile and dynamic learning tools, we integrate digital features such as video, audio, and an online curriculum into one unified and comprehensive course. The result is *Project Success*: the first blended digital course designed for adult-education English language learners.

## MULTIMEDIA: INSIDE AND OUTSIDE THE CLASSROOM

All *Project Success* materials are technologically integrated for seamless independent and classroom learning. The user-friendly digital interface will appeal to students who are already technologically adept, while providing full support for students who have less computer experience.

**In class,** the teacher uses the **Active Teach** DVD-ROM to project the lessons on the board. Video, audio, flashcards, conversation frameworks, checklists, comprehension questions, and other learning material are all available at the click of a button. Students use their print **Student Book** as they participate in class activities, take notes, and interact in group work.

**Outside of class,** students access their *Project Success* **eText** to review the videos, audio, and eFlashcards from class. They use their **MyEnglishLab** access code to get further practice online with new listenings and readings, additional practice activities, and video-based exercises.

## A VARIETY OF WORKFORCE AND LIFE SKILLS

Each level of *Project Success* presents a different cast of characters at a different workplace. In each book, students learn instrumental language, employment, and educational skills as they watch the characters interact with co-workers, customers, family, and friends. As students move through the series, level by level, they learn about six important sectors in today's economy: food service, hospitality, healthcare, higher education, business, and retail.

The language and skills involved in daily life range from following directions, to phone conversations, to helping customers, to asking permission to leave early. By representing a day in the life of a character, *Project Success* can introduce a diverse sampling of the content, language, and competencies involved in daily life and work. This approach allows students to learn diverse competencies and then practice them, in different settings and contexts, at different points in the curriculum.

## VIDEO VIGNETTES

Each unit is organized around a series of short videos that follow one main character through his or her workday. In listening and speaking lessons, students watch the video together, see the character model a key competency in a realistic setting, and then practice the competency in pairs and groups. Discussion questions and group activities encourage students to identify and interpret the rich cultural content embedded in the video. The unit's grammar points are presented in the context of natural language in the video and then highlighted for more study and practice in a separate grammar lesson.

## CRITICAL THINKING SKILLS

In the *What do you think?* activity at the end of nearly every lesson, students analyze, evaluate, infer, or relate content in the lesson to other contexts and situations.

## A ROBUST ASSESSMENT STRAND

The series includes a rich assessment package that consists of unit review tests, midterms, and a CASAS-like final test. The tests assess students on CASAS objectives which are integrated into practical skills and listening strands.

The tests are available online or in a printable version on the ActiveTeach.

## THE COMPONENTS:

### Active Teach

This is a powerful digital platform for teachers. It blends a digital form of the Student Book with interactive whiteboard (IWB) software and printable support materials.

### MyEnglishLab

This is a dynamic, easy-to-use online learning and assessment program that is integral to the *Project Success* curriculum. Original interactive activities extend student practice of vocabulary, listening, speaking, pronunciation, grammar, reading, writing, and practical skills from the classroom learning component.

### eText

The eText is a digital version of the Student Book with all the audio and video integrated, and with a complete set of pop-up eFlashcards.

## WELCOME TO *PROJECT SUCCESS*!

*Project Success* is a six-level digital and print English program designed for you. It teaches English, employment, and learning skills for your success at work and school.

## YOUR CLASSROOM LEARNING

Bring the Student Book to your classroom to learn new material and to practice with your classmates in groups. Every unit has:

- Three video-based lessons for your listening and speaking skills
- One practical skills lesson
- Two grammar lessons
- One lesson for getting a job
- One lesson for writing
- One lesson for reading
- One review page

## YOUR ONLINE LEARNING

Your access code is on the front cover of your Student Book. Use the access code to go online. There you will find eText and MyEnglishLab.

Go to your eText to review what you learned in class. You can watch the videos again, listen to audio, and review the Vocabulary Flashcards.

Go to MyEnglishLab online to practice what you learned in class. MyEnglishLab has:

- Extra listening practice
- Extra reading practice
- Extra grammar practice
- Extra writing practice
- Extra practice of vocabulary skills
- Extra practice of practical skills
- Additional video-based exercises
- "Listen and Record," so you can record yourself and listen to your own pronunciation
- Instant feedback
- Extra job-seeking activities

# Welcome Unit

## MEET YOUR CLASSMATES

**A** 🔊 **Listen. Listen and repeat.**

**Gustavo:** Hi. My name is Gustavo.

**Kristina:** Hello, Gustavo. I'm Kristina.

**Gustavo:** Nice to meet you, Kristina.

**Kristina:** Great to meet you, too.

**Gustavo:** Where are you from?

**Kristina:** Russia. How about you?

**Gustavo:** I'm from Brazil.

**B** PAIRS **Practice the conversation. Use your own name and information.**

**C** **Walk around the room. Meet your classmates.**

## TALK ABOUT YOUR GOALS

**A** **Why are you studying English? Check [✓] the boxes.**

☐ to get a new job

☐ to continue my education

☐ to help my child with schoolwork

☐ other goal: _____

**B** GROUPS **Talk about your goals. Do you have any of the same goals?**

## ASK FOR AND GIVE CLARIFICATION

**A** Complete the conversations. Use the sentences from the box.

Could you explain that?
Did you say a pen?
Do you mean first we should work alone?

I'm sorry. What page?
What's the word for this in English?
What I mean is that you shouldn't read aloud.

**1.**

OK, everyone. Ask your partner the questions on page 14.

I'm sorry. I don't understand. *Could you explain that?*

Sure. Turn to page 14. Work in pairs. Ask your partner the questions.

**2.**

Could I borrow a pen, please?

_____

Yes, a pen. Thanks.

**3.**

Excuse me, Sue. _____
_____

That? That's an outlet.

An outlet? Thanks.

**4.**

When you finish, please check your answers with a partner.

Sorry. _____
_____

Yes, that's right.

**5.**

Class, please look at the article on page 8 and read it to yourselves.

Sorry, I don't understand.

_____
_____
Read silently.

**6.**

OK, everyone. Open your books to page 52.

_____

Page 52.

**B** 🔊 Listen and check your answers.

**C** PAIRS Make similar conversations. Use different information.

## LEARN ABOUT *PROJECT SUCCESS*

**A** **Learn about your book.**
1. Look at the cover of your book. What is the title?
2. Look at the inside front cover. Find the access code.
3. Look at page iii. How many units are in your book?
4. Where can you find a list of vocabulary words?

**B** Meet the characters in your book.
They all work at Park View Hospital.

I'm Frank Sánchez. I work in the Food Services department at Park View. I love music, and I play guitar as a hobby.

I'm Susan Kim. I'm an LVN— that's a licensed vocational nurse. In my free time I love to ride my bike and go out dancing.

I'm Biata Nowicki. I'm a ward clerk. I like going out to parties and to football games with my friends.

I'm Alina Morales. I'm a clinical dietitian. My husband and I have four children—all grown. For me, family is the most important thing in life.

I'm Henry Kaita. I'm a registered nurse, or RN, here at Park View. My passion is my work. I love being a nurse!

**4** WELCOME UNIT

# 1 Frank's Short Day

## MY GOALS

- [ ] Make small talk
- [ ] Ask to leave work early
- [ ] Read medicine labels
- [ ] Ask to borrow something
- [ ] Assess my work needs

Go to MyEnglishLab for more practice after each lesson.

**Frank Sánchez**
Frank                          *Today*
I'm about to start my day at Park View Hospital. I hope the day goes smoothly.

### GET READY TO WATCH

Frank and Susan are arriving at work. What are some things coworkers usually say to each other at the start of a workday? What do you say to your coworkers or classmates?

### WATCH

■◀ **Watch the video. Answer the questions.**

1. What topic do Frank and Susan talk about at the beginning of their conversation?

   _____

2. Where are Frank and Susan? _____

3. What food item does Frank first recommend to Susan? _____

4. What does Susan usually eat for breakfast? _____

5. What does Susan decide to eat? _____

### CONVERSATION

**A**  ■◀ **Watch part of the video. Complete the conversation.**

**Frank:** Hey, good morning, Susan!

**Susan:** Morning, Frank!

**Frank:** Beautiful day, isn't it?

**Susan:** Gorgeous. But I heard it's supposed to _____ later.

**Frank:** Oh, no. Well, at least we had good weather over the weekend, for once.

**Susan:** That's true. What a nice _____! It usually rains on my days off.

**Frank:** I know what you mean.

**B**  ◀))) **Listen and repeat.**

**C**  **PAIRS** Practice the conversation. Use your own names.

**D**  **PAIRS** Make similar conversations. Talk about other topics.

---

**Pronunciation Note**

Notice the intonation (the way the voice goes up and down) in these sentences. When we call someone by name, the voice often goes up a little on the name.

◀))) **Listen and repeat.**

Good **mor**ning, **Su**san!

**Mor**ning, **Frank**!

**Say**, **Frank**, what's **good** here?

---

### WHAT DO YOU THINK?

**GROUPS OF 3** When making small talk with someone you don't know well, what are some topics you should avoid? Explain your answer.

## 2 Adverbs of frequency

**STUDY** Adverbs of frequency

| Subject | Adverb | Verb | |
|---|---|---|---|
| Susan | **always** | eats | fruit for breakfast. |

| Subject | *be* | Adverb | |
|---|---|---|---|
| She | is | **rarely** | at work by 6:30. |

See page 155 for a review of the simple present.

| Adverbs of Frequency | |
|---|---|
| always | 100% |
| usually | |
| often | |
| sometimes | |
| rarely | |
| never | 0% |

**Grammar Note**

*Often*, *sometimes*, and *usually* can also start or end a sentence.

## PRACTICE

**A** Complete the sentences with the adverb of frequency and the correct form of the verb.

1. Frank <u>_always arrives_</u> early at the cafeteria.
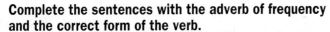
   always / arrive

2. He _____ late to work.
   never / be

3. Susan _____ breakfast at home.
   usually / eat

4. She _____ lunch in the cafeteria.
   often / have

5. The nurses _____ for lunch.
   sometimes / meet

6. The food service workers _____ very busy at lunchtime.
   always / be

**B** Rewrite the sentences on a separate piece of paper. Add the frequency adverbs in parentheses. More than one answer may be possible.

1. (rarely) Susan eats eggs.

> *Susan rarely eats eggs.*

2. (usually) Frank is very hungry in the morning.
3. (often) Teenagers skip breakfast.

4. (rarely) Healthy adults skip breakfast.
5. (never) The cafeteria is open before 6:00.
6. (always) I am up early in the morning.
7. (usually) Frank eats three meals per day.
8. (sometimes) Children need a snack between meals.

## WHAT ABOUT YOU?

**PAIRS** Read the exercise and eating habits in the box. How often do you do each one? Tell your partner. Use complete sentences. Ask follow-up questions to get more information.

| | | | |
|---|---|---|---|
| eat dessert | play a sport | skip a meal | walk to school / work |
| exercise in a gym | ride a bike | snack between meals | |

## Predict the topic

### GET READY

**A**

**Frank is reading an article about breakfast.
How often do you eat the following breakfast foods?**

beans    cereal    eggs    pancakes    rice    bread

**B**

**Read the Reading Skill.
What do you think the article will be about?
Look at the title and the photo and make a prediction.**

> **Reading Skill**
>
> **Making predictions** can help you better understand what you read. You can guess the topic of an article by looking at the title and any subtitles, pictures, and charts.

### READ

🔊 **Listen and read the article. Was your prediction correct?**

# BREAKFAST:
*The Most Important Meal of the Day*

Watching the news one evening, Maria Campos heard some startling information: Skipping breakfast could potentially make you gain weight. "I called my friend Christina right away," she said. "A few months before, we had both decided to go on a diet. We started skipping breakfast to cut calories, but it wasn't working. We didn't lose any weight at all. In fact, we both got a little heavier! Now I understand why."

Skipping breakfast is common. In the U.S., about 10% of the total population, over 31 million people, don't eat breakfast regularly. People give many reasons for skipping breakfast. Like Maria, many do it to lose weight. Some claim they are too rushed in the morning—that they don't have enough time to prepare a meal. Others say that they just don't feel hungry so soon after waking up.

However, research shows that breakfast is more important than people think. "Breakfast gives us the energy we need for our day," says nutritionist Monica Wells. "It helps us concentrate on our work. And it also keeps us from getting hungry. Studies show that people who don't eat breakfast are far more

likely to grab an unhealthy snack before lunch. And this can cause them to put on weight."

According to Ms. Wells, a healthy breakfast doesn't need to be a full meal. It can be as simple as a piece of fruit, a container of low-fat yogurt, and a slice of whole wheat toast with peanut butter. "A few simple 'grab and go' items can provide enough energy to get you through the morning without feeling the urge to snack," says Ms. Wells. "One trick is to include some protein. Protein lasts longer in your body than sugar or carbohydrates, so you don't get hungry as quickly."

So what happened with Maria and Christina? "We went back to eating breakfast," reports Maria. "And we're finally starting to lose weight!"

**U.S.D.A. Healthy Daily Diet**

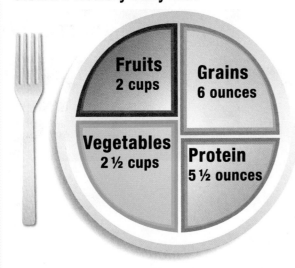

*1 cup = 8 fluid ounces
1 fluid ounce = 0.125 cup
Source: U.S. Department of Agriculture

## AFTER YOU READ

**Look at the chart about healthy daily diets. Answer the questions.**

1. How many cups of vegetables should you eat every day? _____

2. How many ounces of grains should you eat every day? _____

3. Which is larger, 1 cup or 1 ounce? _____

4. Should you eat more vegetables or more fruit every day? _____

## VOCABULARY STUDY  Synonyms

> **Build Your Vocabulary**
>
> A **synonym** is a word that has the same meaning as another word.
> For example, *sad* and *unhappy* are synonyms.
>
> | Synonyms | | | | | |
> |---|---|---|---|---|---|
> | small | – little | large | – big | start | – begin |
> | build | – make | wash | – clean | loud | – noisy |
> | worker | – employee | night | – evening | true | – correct |

**Read the Build Your Vocabulary note. Then read the sentences below.
Find and circle a synonym in the article for each of the underlined words.**

1. Maria learned that not eating breakfast could <u>possibly</u> cause weight gain.

2. Many people say they are too <u>busy</u> in the morning to eat breakfast.

3. People who skip breakfast usually <u>reach for</u> a candy bar before lunch.

4. Maria <u>says</u> that she has started to eat breakfast again.

## WHAT DO YOU THINK?

**GROUPS OF 3**  Talk about what you eat for breakfast. How
healthy is your usual breakfast, according to the article?

> **ON THE WEB**
>
> For more information, go online and
> search "quick healthy breakfast."
> Find a healthy breakfast food that
> you would like to try and report
> back to the class.

## 4

## Ask to leave work early

## GET READY TO WATCH

Frank is asking his supervisor for permission to leave work early today. Have you ever asked to leave work or class early? What was your reason?

## WATCH

■◀ **Watch the video. Answer the questions.**

1. Why does Frank need to leave work early today?

2. What does his supervisor ask him to do before he leaves?

3. Who is going to do Frank's work today while he is out?

## CONVERSATION

**A** ■◀ **Watch part of the video.**
**Complete the conversation.**

**Frank:** Excuse me. Jae?

**Jae:** Hi, Frank. What can I do for you?

**Frank:** Could I possibly leave a little early today?

**Jae:** Today?

**Frank:** Yes, I have a kind of emergency at

_____. The ceiling in my apartment is leaking.

**Jae:** Oh, no. What a pain.

**Frank:** Yeah. My landlord just called. I'm afraid some of my _____ is getting wet. I want to go home and make sure everything is OK.

**Jae:** Of course. I understand.

| Pronunciation Note |
| --- |

Important words in a sentence are stressed. We make them longer and louder. Words like *a*, *the*, *of*, and *at* are usually weak, or *un*stressed. We say them quickly and quietly.

◀))) **Listen and repeat.**
I **have** a **kind** of em**er**gency at **home**.
The **ceil**ing has a **leak**.
**Some** of the **fur**niture is **get**ting **wet**.

**B** ◀))) **Listen and repeat.**

**C** PAIRS **Practice the conversation. Use your own names.**

**D** PAIRS **What are some other reasons for leaving work early?**

*Your child is sick and needs to be picked up at school.*

**E** PAIRS **Make similar conversations. Use your ideas from Exercise D.**

## WHAT DO YOU THINK?

GROUPS OF 3 Frank asked to leave early because of a problem in his apartment. Do you think this is a good reason to leave work early?

## Quantifiers

### STUDY  Quantifier + *of* + specific noun

| Quantifier | *of* | Specific Count Noun | | |
|---|---|---|---|---|
| A few | of | our things | are | damaged. |
| Many | | | | |

| Quantifier | *of* | Specific Count or Noncount Noun | | |
|---|---|---|---|---|
| All | of | the neighbors | are | helping. |
| A lot | | | | |
| Most | | the furniture | is | getting wet. |
| Some | | | | |
| None | | | | |

See page 155 for a list of common quantifiers.

### PRACTICE

**A**  Complete the sentences with the quantifier and the correct noncount or plural count form of the noun. Add *of* and *the* if necessary.

1. ____Most of the patients____ in Frank's wing ate lunch at noon.
   Most / patient

2. Frank is proud because _____ he serves is delicious.
   all / food

3. _____ Frank's _____ are sometimes late.
   A few            coworker

4. _____ Frank serves are hot, and he needs to serve them immediately.
   Some / meal

5. Frank always tastes _____ to be sure it is fresh.
   a little / food

6. Frank hopes that _____ find anything to complain about.
   none / patient

**B**  Write sentences with quantifiers. Use the words in parentheses and a separate piece of paper.

1. (All / the food / at Frank's cafeteria / fresh)

   > All of the food at Frank's cafeteria is fresh.

2. (None / the food / old)
3. (All / Frank's coworkers / friendly)
4. (Some / the new menu items /  not very popular)
5. (A few / the chairs / in the cafeteria / broken)

### WHAT ABOUT YOU?

**PAIRS**  Talk about your class and classmates. Make sentences using quantifiers.

*All of my classmates are friendly.*

## Describe a problem

**GET READY**

**PAIRS** Frank wrote an email to his supervisor to describe a problem at work. Have you ever needed to report a problem at your work or school? What was the problem? Did you offer a solution?

**STUDY THE MODEL**

**A** Read Frank's email. What problem does Frank describe? What solution does Frank suggest to help fix the problem?

---

**From:** Frank Sánchez
**To:** Jae Park
**Subject:** Employee training

---

Hi Jae,

I'm writing to make a suggestion about employee training. I think that the food service department needs more training sessions. We always train new staff, but I think we should offer regular training to everyone. This will help us refresh our skills and learn new skills.

I'm suggesting this because I see some problems with the food service these days. Staff members are not following our basic food service guidelines. One problem is that some staff members are not being careful with food portions. So some patients are getting too much food, and other patients are getting too little. Also, we are often late when we clear away the trays after lunch. Two of the patients complained about this to me today.

I think that regular refresher training sessions will help us provide better customer service. I could help prepare the session or even lead it. What do you think? I am working all day tomorrow, so maybe we can talk more about it then.

Regards,

Frank

Frank Sánchez
Patient Dining Assistant
Park View Hospital
Houston, TX

---

**B** Read the Writing Tip. Then read Frank's email again. Underline two examples that show why Frank's department needs a training session.

**C** Look at the ideas web Frank used to organize his ideas. Complete the ideas web with the missing information.

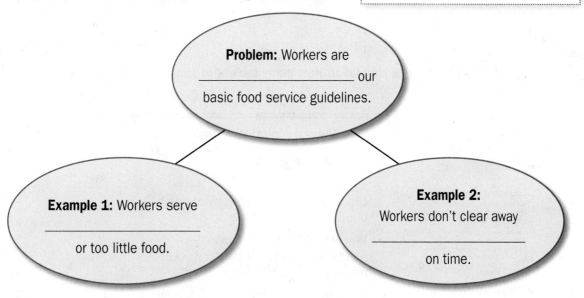

**Problem:** Workers are _____ our basic food service guidelines.

**Example 1:** Workers serve _____ or too little food.

**Example 2:** Workers don't clear away _____ on time.

## BEFORE YOU WRITE

You're going to write an email describing a problem in your workplace, school, or community. Create an ideas web to plan your email. Use a separate piece of paper if necessary.

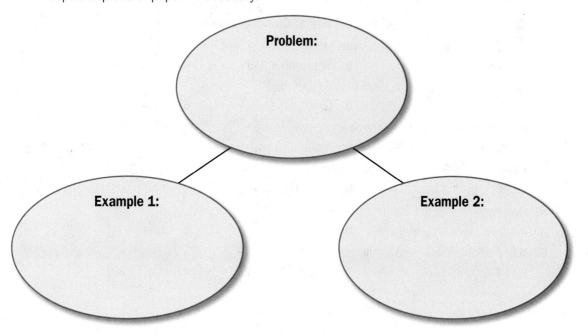

**Problem:**

**Example 1:**

**Example 2:**

## WRITE

Review the model and the Writing Tip. Use the ideas in your web to write your email.

# Read medicine labels

 **GET READY**

Frank is in the hospital pharmacy getting some prescription medicine and some over-the-counter (OTC) medicine. What are some differences between prescription and OTC medication?

 **PRACTICAL READING**

**A** Read the prescription medicine label. How many tablets of Timodol did Frank get?

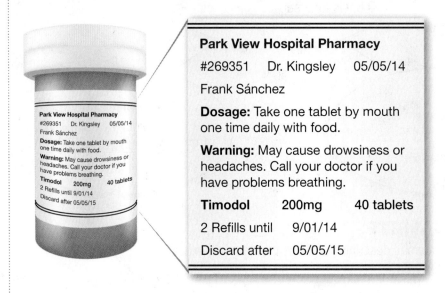

**Park View Hospital Pharmacy**

#269351    Dr. Kingsley    05/05/14

Frank Sánchez

**Dosage:** Take one tablet by mouth one time daily with food.

**Warning:** May cause drowsiness or headaches. Call your doctor if you have problems breathing.

**Timodol**      200mg          40 tablets

2 Refills until      9/01/14

Discard after      05/05/15

**B** Read the prescription medicine label again. Circle the correct answers.

1. What is the date Frank got his medicine?
   a. May 5             b. September 1         c. December 31

2. How many tablets should Frank take each day?
   a. one               b. two                 c. three

3. How can this medicine affect your body?
   a. it can keep you awake   b. it can give you energy   c. it can make you sleepy

4. When should Frank call his doctor?
   a. if he gets a headache   b. if he feels tired   c. if he has trouble breathing

5. How many refills did the doctor prescribe?
   a. one               b. two                 c. three

6. When should Frank throw this medicine away?
   a. May 5, 2014       b. September 1, 2014   c. May 5, 2015

**C**  Read the OTC medicine label. What is this medicine for?

## Abater

Ibuprofen capsules   200 mg   Exp. date: 03/17
Pain Reliever / Fever Reducer                100 caps
Active ingredient (in each capsule):
Ibuprofen 200 mg
**Purpose:** Pain reliever / fever reducer
**Uses:**

Relieves pain from:
- fever
- muscle ache
- backache
- colds

**Warnings** May cause allergic reaction. Stop use immediately and see a doctor if you develop a rash.

Keep out of reach of children.

**Directions** Adults and children 12 years take 1 capsule every 4 to 6 hours; if pain persists, take 2 capsules, but do not take more than 6 capsules in 24 hours

Children under 12 years: Ask a doctor.

**D**  Read the OTC medicine label again. Complete the sentences.

1. There are _____ capsules in this bottle.

2. You should call the doctor if you get a _____.

3. If the pain continues, you can take _____ capsules at a time.

4. You should not take more than _____ capsules per day.

5. If you take this medicine at 3:00, the earliest time you can take it again is _____.

## PRACTICAL LISTENING

**A**   Frank is listening to a podcast about prescription medication. What does the doctor warn patients not to do?

**B**   Listen again. Read the statements. Circle *True* or *False*, according to the information in the podcast. Then correct the false statements.

1. It's OK to borrow another person's medication if that person is a family member.                                                                     True      False

2. Prescription drugs affect everyone the same way.                          True      False

3. Doctors may look at a patient's weight before choosing a dosage.          True      False

4. If you borrow someone else's medication, you may not understand how to take it safely.                                                             True      False

5. If you use a prescription drug without a doctor's prescription, you are breaking the law.                                                          True      False

## WHAT DO YOU THINK?

**GROUPS OF 3** Frank forgot to refill his prescription in time. Now it's dinner time, and he needs to take his medicine, but the bottle is empty. What should he do?

# LISTENING AND SPEAKING

## Ask to borrow something

## GET READY TO WATCH

Frank is going to borrow Amber's cell phone. In what situations do you borrow someone else's phone?

## WATCH

◼◀ **Watch the video. Answer the questions.**

1. Why can't Frank use his own phone?
2. Who does Frank call?
3. What does Frank have to send?
4. What item does Frank forget to return to Amber?

## CONVERSATION

**A** ◼◀ **Watch part of the video. Complete the conversation.**

**Frank:** Hi, Amber. Can I ask you a favor?

**Amber:** Sure. What is it?

**Frank:** _____ I borrow your phone for a minute? My battery is dead.

**Amber:** No problem. Here you go.

**Frank:** Thanks. My apartment has some water damage.

I _____ call my insurance company.

**Amber:** That's fine.

**B** ◀)) **Listen and repeat.**

**C** **PAIRS** Practice the conversation. Use your own names.

**D** **PAIRS** Think about other situations in which you might ask to borrow something. What do you ask to borrow? Why do you need or want it?

*I ask to borrow an umbrella from my coworker because it's raining.*
*I want to get lunch, but I forgot my umbrella at home.*

**E** **PAIRS** Make similar conversations. Ask to borrow other things. Use your ideas from Exercise D. Give reasons using "I have to" or "I want to."

## WHAT DO YOU THINK?

**GROUPS OF 3** Would you ever allow a stranger to use your cell phone? Why or why not?

# JOB-SEEKING SKILLS

## Assess your work needs

**Mario López** *Today*
Hi! I'm Frank's cousin. I just moved here, and I need a job. I'm a licensed vocational nurse (LVN).

### GET READY

Mario is thinking about his job needs. What do you need to think about before you can find a job? What questions might you ask yourself?

### ASSESS YOUR WORK NEEDS

**A** ◀)) **Listen to Mario talk about his work needs. Answer the questions.**

1. Does Mario want a full-time job or a part-time job? _____

2. What kind of training does Park View offer for LVNs? _____

3. At which location does Mario want to work? _____

4. How does Mario feel about being on his feet a lot? _____

5. Does Mario prefer to work with people, or with computers? _____

**B** ◀)) **Mario is completing a chart with the job features he wants. Listen again and complete the chart.**

| Do you want . . . | |
|---|---|
| _____ a part-time job? | _____ a full-time job? |
| _____ a morning shift _____ an afternoon shift _____ an evening shift _____ a night shift | |
| _____ a job that requires training? | _____ a job that provides training? |
| _____ a job you can drive to? | _____ a job near a bus / train stop? |
| _____ a job where you can sit a lot? | _____ a job where you can be active? |
| _____ a job working with people? | _____ a job working with computers? |
| _____ a job working inside? | _____ a job working outside? |
| _____ a job working with your hands? | _____ a job that requires decision-making skills? |

**C** ◀)) **Mario continues talking to his friend about his work needs. Listen and answer the questions.**

1. How much money does Mario want to earn per hour? _____

2. What kind of benefits does Mario want? Check [✓] all the correct answers.

   ☐ health insurance    ☐ dental insurance    ☐ life insurance

   ☐ retirement savings program    ☐ vacation time    ☐ sick time

## PUT YOUR IDEAS TO WORK

**A** **Imagine that you are looking for a job. Complete the chart in Exercise B and the questions in Exercise C with your own job needs.**

**B** **PAIRS** Compare your job features charts. Talk about your job needs. Which job features *must* you have? Which would you *like* to have?

# UNIT 1 REVIEW

## GRAMMAR

In this unit, you studied:
- Adverbs of frequency
- Quantifier + *of* + specific noun

See page 145 for your Grammar Review.

## VOCABULARY  See page 162 for the Unit 1 Vocabulary.

**Vocabulary Learning Strategy: Draw Pictures**

**A** Choose five words or expressions from the Unit 1 Word List. In your notebook, draw pictures of each word. Write the words next to each picture.

**B** Write a sentence with each word in Exercise A.

a leak

## SPELLING  See page 162 for the Unit 1 Vocabulary.

**CLASS** Choose ten words for a spelling test.

## LISTENING PLUS

**A** Watch each video. Write the story of Frank's day.

> Frank met his coworker Susan at the start of work. They made small talk and Frank recommended some food for breakfast.

**B** **PAIRS** Review the Lesson 4 conversation. See page 10. **Role play the conversation for the class.**

## NOW I CAN

**PAIRS** See page 5 for the Unit 1 Goals.  Check ✔ the things you can do. Underline the things you want to study more. Tell your partner.

> I can _____. I need more practice with _____.

# 2 Biata's Crazy Day

## MY GOALS

- ☐ Call in late
- ☐ Ask for help
- ☐ Read a street map
- ☐ Give directions
- ☐ Assess my job skills

Go to MyEnglishLab for more practice after each lesson.

**Biata Nowick**

**Biata**                    *Today*
Life as a hospital receptionist is always busy, busy, busy! And I like it that way. ☺

## Call in late

### GET READY TO WATCH

Biata is calling in late to work. Have you ever had to call someone to say you would be late? What was your reason?

### WATCH

■◀ **Watch the video. Circle the correct answers.**

1. Why is Biata late?
   a. Her car won't start.
   b. There is a lot of traffic.
   c. She missed the bus.

2. When does Biata think she can be at work?
   a. by 9 o'clock
   b. by 10 o'clock
   c. by 11 o'clock

3. What does Ida ask Biata to do?
   a. work extra hours
   b. cover for Jimmy
   c. drive carefully

4. What does Biata have to do at work later?
   a. go to a meeting for Ida
   b. take notes about the accident
   c. make plans with Bay Side

### CONVERSATION

**A** ■◀ **Watch part of the video. Complete the conversation.**

**Biata:** Hi Ida, it's Biata.

**Ida:** Oh, good morning, Biata.

**Biata:** Good morning. I'm _____, but I'm afraid I'm going to be a little late today.

**Ida:** Oh? Is everything okay?

**Biata:** Yes, everything is fine. I'm just stuck in traffic. I haven't moved in ten minutes.

**Ida:** Oh, I see.

**Biata:** It looks like there was an accident or something.

**Ida:** OK. Well, _____ for letting me know. How soon do you think you'll be here?

**Biata:** I think by 10 o'clock.

> **Pronunciation Note**
>
> Pronouns, and contractions with a pronoun, are usually unstressed.
>
> ◀)) **Listen and repeat. Notice the short, weak pronunciation of the contractions with *be* and *will*.**
>
> I'm **sorry**, but I'm **afraid** I'm **going** to be a little **late today**.
>
> **How soon do** you **think** you'll be **here?**
>
> I'll **be there** as soon as I can.

**B** ◀)) **Listen and repeat.**

**C** **PAIRS** **Practice the conversation. Use your own names.**

**D** **PAIRS** **Make similar conversations. Use other reasons for being late.**

### WHAT DO YOU THINK?

**GROUPS OF 3** Do you think Biata acted appropriately in her situation? Explain why or why not. When an employee is late, what does he or she need to do?

# GRAMMAR

## 2 Future forms

 **STUDY** Future forms

| Review: Future with *be going to* and *will* | | |
|---|---|---|
| I **am not going to** be late. | **Are** you **going to** be here soon? | Yes, I am. / No, I'm not. |
| We **will** help you tomorrow. | How late **will** you stay? | Until 5:30. |

| Present Continuous with Future Meaning | | |
|---|---|---|
| I **am working** tomorrow. | **Are** you **working** on Friday? | Yes, I am. / No, I'm not. |
| We **are not meeting** at 1:00. | When **are** we **meeting**? | At 3:00. |

**Grammar Note**

Use *be going to* or *will* to talk about facts or make predictions about things you are sure will happen in the future.

Use *be going to* or the present continuous to talk about future plans or things you have already decided.

Use *will* for decisions you make while you are speaking or to make offers or promises.

See page 146 for a complete review of future forms.

 **PRACTICE**

**A** **Complete the sentences with the future form in parentheses and the correct form of the verb.**

1. (will) I can't decide which meeting to attend. I think _____*I will go*_____ to the one at 2:00.
   <u>go</u>

2. (pres. cont.) Paulo _____ in late today. He called an hour ago.
   <u>come</u>

3. (will) _____ he _____ here in time for the lunch rounds?
   <u>be</u>

4. (be going to) It's Lila's birthday. The nurses _____ her a gift.
   <u>give</u>

**B** **Complete the conversations with the correct future form of the verb. More than one answer may be possible.**

1. **Nurse A:** Uh-oh. That bottle is too close to the edge of the cart. It's _____*going to fall*_____ off!
   <u>fall</u>

   **Nurse B:** I _____ it for you.
   <u>get</u>

2. **Doctor:** _____ you _____ here when the lab reports arrive?
   <u>be</u>

   **Lab technician:** Yes. We _____ them in about an hour.
   <u>have</u>

3. **Orderly A:** _____ you _____ the big meeting tomorrow?
   <u>attend</u>

   **Orderly B:** No. I _____ here in the morning. I have an appointment.
   <u>not / be</u>

## WHAT ABOUT YOU?

**PAIRS** Talk about your future plans. Use *be going to*, *will*, and the present continuous.

# 3 Skim to find the main idea

## GET READY

Biata read a blog about being late to work. Are you usually on time for work or class?

> **Reading Skill**
>
> **Skimming** is reading something quickly to get the general idea of the text. To skim an article, look at the title and any subtitles. Then read the first sentence in each paragraph.

**Read the Reading Skill. Skim the Internet blog. What is the main idea?**

## READING

◀))) **Listen and read the blog. Was your answer about the main idea correct?**

▶ MY PROFILE   ▶ SUBSCRIBE   ▶ BLOG ARCHIVE

### You're Late Because of *What*?

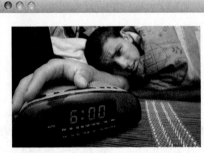

Some people just can't get up in the morning. They hit the snooze button on their alarm clock over and over before they finally roll out of bed. I also have this trouble from time to time, so I'm understanding when my employees arrive a little late to work. In fact, surveys show that 16% of employees are late to work at least once a week.

Of course, everybody has an excuse. I hear the usual explanations often—people get stuck in traffic jams, have sick children, or miss their bus. But I get some weird ones, too! One of my employees was an hour late today. He told me he'd bought a new GPS, and it took him to the wrong address. I wasn't very sympathetic. "Surely you know the way to work after three years," I said. That made me think about the odd excuses I've heard over the years. Here are some of the strangest:

1. "I didn't think you'd notice when I came in."
2. "I ate my wife's breakfast by mistake, so I had to make it again."
3. "I had to go back to change my shoes because I noticed I was wearing two different ones."
4. "The right turn signal of my car wasn't working, so I could only make left turns to get to work."
5. "I had to stop to let a mother duck and her ducklings cross the road. She was not in a hurry."

I think we can all get a good laugh from these excuses. But being on time is important. Come in to work late too often, and you'll make a really bad impression on your boss. I did have to fire someone once for chronic lateness. Thirty-one percent of employers say they've had to do that. So in your own career interest, I recommend getting to work on time. No more excuses!

POSTED BY KKEYES AT 10:58 AM          ✉ Share   👍 Like

## AFTER YOU READ

**Look at the chart about common excuses for being late. Answer the questions on a separate piece of paper.**

1. What is the most common excuse for being late?

2. What percentage of people said they were late because of bad weather?

3. What percentage of people said they were late because of problems with their clothing?

4. Are more people late because of problems with child care or pets?

## VOCABULARY STUDY  Antonyms

**Most Common Excuses for Being Late to Work**

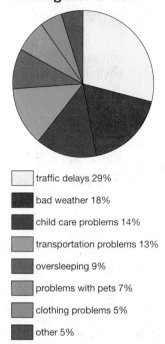

- traffic delays 29%
- bad weather 18%
- child care problems 14%
- transportation problems 13%
- oversleeping 9%
- problems with pets 7%
- clothing problems 5%
- other 5%

### Build Your Vocabulary

An **antonym** is a word that means the opposite of another word. For example, *hot* and *cold* are antonyms.

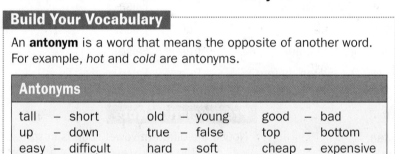

| Antonyms | | | | | |
|---|---|---|---|---|---|
| tall | – short | old | – young | good | – bad |
| up | – down | true | – false | top | – bottom |
| easy | – difficult | hard | – soft | cheap | – expensive |

**Read the Build Your Vocabulary note. Then read the sentences. Find and circle an antonym in the reading for each of the underlined words.**

1. I was <u>early</u> for my appointment with the teacher.

2. He gave a <u>typical</u> reason for wanting to learn English.

3. I believe I dialed the <u>correct</u> phone number.

4. Martin and I have <u>the same</u> teacher this semester.

## WHAT DO YOU THINK?

**ON THE WEB**

For more information, go online and search "strange reasons for being late." Find three new strange reasons for being late for work and report back to the class.

**A** **Imagine that you are a manager. Look at the excuses for being late to work. Decide which ones are acceptable (A) and which ones are not acceptable (NA).**

1. _____ I wanted to finish reading a very exciting book.

2. _____ There was a traffic jam on my way in to work.

3. _____ I had to drive my spouse to work today.

4. _____ I had to help my sister with her homework because she forgot to do it last night.

5. _____ I thought it was a holiday today.

**B** **PAIRS Compare your answers in Exercise A. Explain your reasons.**

**C** **GROUPS OF 3 Talk about the most unusual reason you have been late somewhere.**

## Ask for help

## GET READY TO WATCH

Biata is having trouble with some computer software. Have you ever had problems using a computer? What did you do?

## WATCH

■◀ **Watch the video. Read the statements. Circle *True* or *False*. Correct the false statements.**

| | | |
|---|---|---|
| 1. Biata is having trouble using the patient database. | True | False |
| 2. She can't enter the patient information. | True | False |
| 3. Biata has been using the wrong computer. | True | False |
| 4. Jimmy also had trouble with the system before. | True | False |

## CONVERSATION

Ⓐ ■◀ **Watch part of the video. Complete the conversation.**

**Biata:** I'm having some _____ with the new patient database. Can you help me?

**Jimmy:** Of course. What's the problem?

**Biata:** Well, I entered the patient data, but I wasn't able to save the information.

**Jimmy:** Really? Did you click on the "save" icon?

**Biata:** I did. But it didn't save the data.

**Jimmy:** Huh. That's _____. I'll come by in a few minutes and take a look.

**Biata:** Great! Thank you.

Ⓑ ◀)) **Listen and repeat.**

Ⓒ **PAIRS Practice the conversation.**

Ⓓ **PAIRS Make similar conversations. Use other problems.**

### Pronunciation Note

Notice the different vowel sounds in *save* /eɪ/ and *well* /ɛ/. The sound /eɪ/ (*save*) is a long sound.

◀)) **Listen and repeat.**

| /eɪ/ | save | able | great | patient | database |
|---|---|---|---|---|---|
| /ɛ/ | well | get | help | enter | remember |

## WHAT DO YOU THINK?

**GROUPS OF 3** Imagine that someone you work with is always asking you for help, and you are having trouble getting your own work done. What can you do?

# 5

## Past ability

### STUDY Past ability with *be able to* and *could*

**be able to: Statements**

| Subject | be | (not) able to | Base Form of Verb | |
|---|---|---|---|---|
| Biata | was | not able to | open | the file. |

| Yes/No Questions | Short Answers |
|---|---|
| **Was** she **able to help** you? | Yes, she was. / No, she wasn't. |
| **Were** you **able to fix** it? | Yes, I was. / No, I wasn't. |

**could: Statements**

| Subject | could (not) | Base Form of Verb | |
|---|---|---|---|
| I | could not | see | the icon. |

| Yes/No Questions | Short Answers |
|---|---|
| **Could** you **finish** everything? | Yes, I could. / No, I couldn't. |

**Grammar Note**

Use *was / were able to* or *could* for past ability. Do not use *could* in affirmative statements for a single event in the past. You can use *couldn't* for single past events.

### PRACTICE

**A** Complete the sentences with *could* or the correct past form of *be able to*. Use affirmative or negative forms.

**1.** Victor _____was able to_____ use the new database. He didn't have any trouble.
    <sub>be able to</sub>

**2.** Finally, we _____ enter the information. It took a long time!
    <sub>be able to</sub>

**3.** Biata _____ finish the reports. She didn't have time.
    <sub>be able to</sub>

**4.** Jimmy _____ take a break. He was too busy.
    <sub>could</sub>

**B** Complete the conversations with *could* or the correct past form of *be able to* and the verb. More than one answer may be possible.

**Ida:** _____Were you able to enter_____ all of the patient information?
    <sub>1. enter</sub>

**Biata:** No. I _____. I'll ask Layla to help.
    <sub>2. finish</sub>

**Ida:** And _____ the insurance companies?
    <sub>3. call</sub>

**Biata:** Yes, I _____ all of them.
    <sub>4. call</sub>

### WHAT ABOUT YOU?

**PAIRS** What can you do now that you couldn't do in the past?

# Give instructions

 **GET READY**

Biata wasn't able to finish a task she was working on. She wrote a note to her coworker, Layla, on the next shift. Have you ever needed to ask someone to finish a job for you? How did you explain the task to the other person?

 **STUDY THE MODEL**

**A** **Read Biata's note. What does Biata need Layla to do?**

☐ attend a meeting ☐ enter information into a database

☐ talk to patients about their medical history

> Layla —
>
> Ida asked me to go to the meeting about the plans with Bay Side. I wasn't able to finish entering the patient information into the database, so I need you to work on this. The unfinished charts are next to the computer. Here's how you enter the information for each chart:
>
> First of all, open the database software. (It's the icon on the left, named "Patient Records.") Then click on "New Patient" at the top left of the screen. It opens up a new patient file. Next, enter the patient's personal information on screen 1 of the patient's file. (Remember to click on "Save"!) On screen 2, enter the patient's medical history. And on screen 3, enter the patient's insurance information. Finally, click on "Submit" and you're finished. Please file the finished charts alphabetically.
>
> If you can't finish all of them, don't worry. I can take care of it tomorrow. Thanks!
> -Biata

**Writing Tip**

When giving instructions, it's important to show the order in which things must be done. Use **transitional phrases** such as *first of all*, *then*, *next*, and *finally* to signal the steps in the process.

**B** **Read the Writing Tip. Then read the note again. Underline four transitional phrases.**

**26** UNIT 2

**C** Look at the flow chart Biata used to plan her note, and complete it.

**Task:** Enter patient information in database

Step 1: _____ the database.

Step 2: Click on "_____."

Step 3: _____ the patient's personal information on Screen 1.

Step 4: Enter the patient's _____ history on Screen 2.

Step 5: Enter the patient's _____ on _____.

Step 6: _____.

Step 7: _____.

## BEFORE YOU WRITE

**A** You're going to ask someone you know to do a task for you.
Think of a task that you need to do. It should have at least three steps.

Task: _____

**B** Create a flow chart for your task. Describe the steps it will take to complete it.
Use a separate piece of paper.

## WRITE

Review the model and the Writing Tip. Write a note to someone you know. Ask him or her to do the task for you. Use your chart to explain the steps the person needs to take.

## GET READY

Biata has to take the bus to work tomorrow. She is checking a map so she knows where the bus station is. How often do you use street maps? Where can you find them?

## PRACTICAL READING

**A** Match the words from the box with the abbreviations.

| | | | | | | | |
|---|---|---|---|---|---|---|---|
| **a.** | Avenue | **d.** | Freeway | **g.** | Route | **j.** | South |
| **b.** | Boulevard | **e.** | Highway | **h.** | Street | **k.** | East |
| **c.** | Drive | **f.** | Road | **i.** | North | **l.** | West |

1. _____ St.    4. _____ Rd.    7. _____ Blvd.    10. _____ Dr.

2. _____ W     5. _____ N      8. _____ Hwy.    11. _____ E

3. _____ Ave.   6. _____ Fwy.   9. _____ S       12. _____ Rte.

**B** 🔊)) Listen and check your answers.

**C** Look at the street map and legend. Answer the questions.

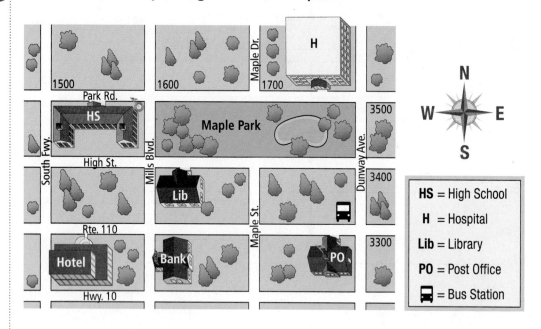

1. What does the map legend show?
   - **a.** addresses of places on the map
   - **b.** what the symbols on the map mean
   - **c.** directions from one place to another
   - **d.** what you can do at different places

2. What does "H" stand for?
   - **a.** high school
   - **b.** hospital
   - **c.** houses
   - **d.** High Street

3. Where is "north" on this map?
   - **a.** at the top
   - **b.** at the bottom
   - **c.** on the left
   - **d.** on the right

4. If you start at the bank and go one block west, what will you find?
   - **a.** the bus station
   - **b.** the post office
   - **c.** the library
   - **d.** a hotel

**D** **PAIRS** Take turns. Talk about the places on the map in Exercise C. Say where each place is. Use the numbers on the map to give an exact address, or say the street name and the cross-street.

*The high school is at 1500 Park Road, between South Freeway and Mills Boulevard.*

## PRACTICAL LISTENING

◀))) **Look at the map. Listen. Where are the places located on the map? Write the correct letter on the line.**

1. hospital _____

2. children's museum _____

3. library _____

4. bike shop _____

5. school _____

6. bus stop _____

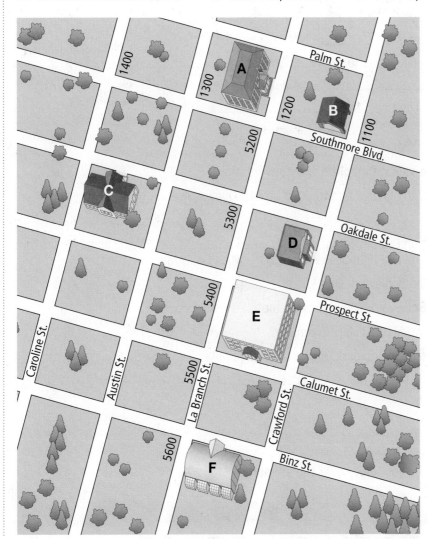

## WHAT DO YOU THINK?

**GROUPS OF 3** Many people have GPS devices in their cars and on their cell phones that can give accurate directions to any address. Do you think that we still need paper maps?

8

## Give directions

### GET READY TO WATCH

Biata is giving directions to a patient's relative. When was the last time you needed to ask for directions? Who did you ask? Were the directions helpful?

### WATCH

■◀ **Watch the video. Complete the sentences.**

1. The man's _____ is a patient at the hospital.

2. The man asks if there is a _____ nearby.

3. Biata gives the man directions to the West Park _____.

4. The park is on the _____ side of the street.

5. The shopping mall is just past the _____.

### CONVERSATION

**A** ■◀ **Watch part of the video. Complete the conversation.**

**Biata:** Drive out of the garage and turn left. That's Dunway Avenue.

**Mr. Galvis:** All right.

**Biata:** Go straight on Dunway for about five _____. You'll come to a traffic light. Take a right at the light. That's Mills Boulevard.

**Mr. Galvis:** Right at Mills Boulevard. OK.

**Biata:** Yes. Mills Boulevard. The mall is on that _____.

**Mr. Galvis:** How far down Mills Boulevard do I go?

**Biata:** Not far. You'll see the park on your left. The mall is just past that,

on the same side of the _____.

**B** ◀⟩⟩ **Listen and repeat.**

**C** PAIRS **Practice the conversation.**

**D** PAIRS **Make similar conversations.**
**Give directions to places you know near the school.**

## WHAT DO YOU THINK?

GROUPS OF 3 Imagine that you are driving in a new area and you get lost. What do you think is the best way to get directions?

# JOB-SEEKING SKILLS
## Assess your job skills

Mario López    *Today*
I may not have a job, but I've been working hard! Today I'm figuring out what my skills are.

## GET READY

Frank's cousin Mario wants to assess his job skills before he begins looking for a job. Why is it important to understand what you do well?

## ASSESS YOUR JOB SKILLS

**A** ◀))) **Mario attended a job-training workshop about assessing job skills. Listen to the first part of the workshop. What is a "hard" skill, according to the speaker?**

**B** **Look at the chart that Mario completed about his hard skills. What skill did Mario use at Medical City Hospital?**

| Hard Skill | Example |
|---|---|
| type 45 words a minute | Keystone Temp Agency |
| use computer software | Keystone Temp Agency |
| provide basic nursing care | LVN at Medical City Hospital |
| speak English and Spanish | various |

**C** ◀))) **Listen to the second part of the workshop. Why does the speaker think that "soft" skills are important?**

## PUT YOUR IDEAS TO WORK

**A** **Look at the Soft Skills Assessment Survey. Check [✓] the soft skills you are good at or enjoy doing. For each skill you check, think of a time when you used this skill. Then write a skill you have that is not on the list.**

### Soft Skills Assessment Survey

- ☐ work under stress
- ☐ adapt to new situations
- ☐ learn from criticism
- ☐ work well with others
- ☐ solve problems
- ☐ work with your hands
- ☐ care for young children

- ☐ be a good listener
- ☐ manage time efficiently
- ☐ communicate ideas clearly
- ☐ sell a product or idea
- ☐ have a positive attitude
- ☐ think of creative ideas
- ☐ negotiate with others

- ☐ multi-task
- ☐ teach / train others
- ☐ learn new things
- ☐ show leadership
- ☐ organize information
- ☐ have a sense of humor
- ☐ provide customer service

Other: _____

**B** **PAIRS** **Talk about your hard and soft skills. Give examples of times when you used these skills at work or in your life.**

## GRAMMAR

In this unit, you studied:
- Future forms
- Past ability with *be able to* and *could*

See page 146 for your Grammar Review.

## VOCABULARY  See page 162 for the Unit 2 Vocabulary.

### Vocabulary Learning Strategy: Group by Meanings

A  Choose words from the Unit 2 Word List and put them into these groups.

| Maps | Computers | Job Skills |
|---|---|---|
| a block | a database | multi-task |
| | | |
| | | |
| | | |
| | | |

B  Circle five words in Exercise A. Write a sentence with each word.

## SPELLING  See page 162 for the Unit 2 Vocabulary.

CLASS  Choose ten words for a spelling test.

## LISTENING PLUS

A  Watch each video. Write the story of Biata's day.

Biata had some trouble this morning. She got stuck in traffic and was
late to work.

B  PAIRS  Review the Lesson 8 conversation. See page 30. Role play the
conversation for the class.

## NOW I CAN

PAIRS  See page 19 for the Unit 2 Goals.  Check ☑ the things you can do.
Underline the things you want to study more. Tell your partner.

I can _____. I need more practice with _____.

# 3

# Susan's Cares and Concerns

## MY GOALS

☐ Talk about things I used to do

☐ Talk about workplace safety

☐ Report an accident

☐ Ask for and give clarification

☐ Read a job ad

Go to MyEnglishLab for more practice after each lesson.

**Park View Hospital**
Susan Kim
Licensed Vocational Nurse
LVN

Susan Kim
Susan    Today
I love my job as a
Licensed Vocational Nurse.
Encouraging patients is my
favorite part of the job.

33

# LISTENING AND SPEAKING

## 1 Talk about things you used to do

### GET READY TO WATCH

Mrs. Richards's granddaughter is going to have a baby. Guess. What is Susan telling Mrs. Richards?

### WATCH

**A** ▪◀ **Watch the video. Was your guess correct?**

**B** ▪◀ **Watch the video again. Circle the correct answers.**

1. Mrs. Richards was _____ about having her first baby.
   **a.** calm          **b.** difficult          **c.** nervous

2. Mrs. Richards says her granddaughter can _____ to get information easily.
   **a.** go online          **b.** ask the doctor          **c.** read a book

3. Mrs. Richards also thinks things are _____ now.
   **a.** more comfortable          **b.** safer          **c.** more convenient

4. Mrs. Richards plans to stay with her granddaughter for _____.
   **a.** a week          **b.** two weeks          **c.** one month

### CONVERSATION

**A** ▪◀ **Watch part of the video. Complete the conversation.**

**Mrs. Richards:** Of course, things were _____ back then.

**Susan:** I can imagine!

**Mrs. Richards:** For one thing, we didn't use to have so much _____.
Nowadays, you can just go online and find out anything you want to know.

**Susan:** That's true.

**Mrs. Richards:** And things are _____these days, too.

**Susan:** What do you mean?

**Mrs. Richards:** Well, for example, children use car seats now.
We used to just carry babies in our laps!

**B** ◀))) **Listen and repeat.**

**C** **PAIRS Practice the conversation.**

**D** **PAIRS Talk about the changes that have happened in your lifetime. How are things more convenient now than in the past? How are things more difficult?**

**E** **SAME PAIRS Make similar conversations. Use your ideas from Exercise D.**

> **Pronunciation Note**
>
> We usually pronounce both *used to* and *use to* as "useta."
>
> ◀))) **Listen and repeat.**
> We used to carry babies in our laps.
>
> We didn't even use to wear seat belts.

## WHAT DO YOU THINK?

**GROUPS OF 3** Can you think of other examples of how things are safer now than in the past?

# 2  *Used to*

## STUDY  *Used to*

### Statements

| Subject | *used to/not use to* | Base Form of Verb | |
|---|---|---|---|
| I | used to | carry | my baby in my lap. |
| We | didn't use to | have | car seats. |

| Questions | Short Answers |
|---|---|
| **Did** you **use to share** hospital rooms? | Yes, we did. / No, we didn't. |
| **How many** nurses **used to work** in the OR? | I'm not sure. Maybe ten. |

### Grammar Note

Use *used to* for past habits that have changed.
The form of *used to* is the same for all subject nouns and pronouns.
Note the spelling of *use to* for negative statements and questions with *did*.

See page 157 for a review of the simple past.

## PRACTICE

**A**  **Complete the sentences with the correct form of *used to*.**

1. Many child safety items exist today that mothers didn't _____*use to*_____ have.

2. In the 1980s, children _____ get four different vaccinations.

3. Doctors _____ visit patients at home more often.

4. We didn't _____ use so many disposable diapers.

5. Baby bottles _____ be made of glass.

6. Parents _____ allow babies to sleep on sofas, chairs, or regular beds.

7. Now we always remove pillows, blankets, and toys from a baby's crib. We didn't _____ do that.

**B**  **Frank tells Susan about changes at Park View Hospital. Complete their conversation with the correct form of *used to* and the verb.**

**Frank:**  Park View Hospital ____*used to be*____ a small hospital. It _____
                                    1. be                                                              2. have
only 200 beds.

**Susan:**  Oh, really? _____ it _____ a maternity department?
                                                        3. have

**Frank:**  Yes. But there _____ a children's department. They built that in 1980.
                              4. not / be

**Susan:**  How many people _____ here back then?
                                        5. work

**Frank:**  I'm not sure. But in food services, there _____ ten of us.
                                                                6. be

## WHAT ABOUT YOU?

**PAIRS**  What are some activities that you used to do as a child that you no longer do?
What are some things you do now that you didn't use to do?

# 3

## Talk about workplace safety

### GET READY

Susan's hospital has safety notices to help workers avoid injuries.
What do you think are some safety issues at a hospital?

### PRACTICAL READING

**A** **Read the safety notice. What is a common cause of workplace injuries, according to the safety notice?**

☐ packing boxes too heavy ☐ lifting the wrong way ☐ not wearing safety glasses

---

### AVOID WORKPLACE INJURY
### KNOW HOW TO LIFT PROPERLY!

Many workplace injuries are caused by lifting heavy objects the **WRONG** way. Learn how to lift the **RIGHT** way to avoid these common injuries. Only **YOU** can keep yourself safe when lifting.

**1. Examine the object.**
- Can you push the object? If you can push it, you can lift it. If you cannot push it, do not lift it. Get help.
- Does the object have handles? Before you lift it, think about the best place to position your hands.

**2. Position yourself.**
- Stand with your feet shoulder-width apart. Squat down. Keep your back straight. Tuck in your chin.
- If necessary, put one knee on the floor and your other knee in front of you, bent at a right angle (half kneeling).

**3. Lift the object.**
- Grip the object with your hands. Lift the object as you straighten your legs.
- Use your leg muscles, not your back muscles. Do not twist as you lift.
- Keep your chest out and your shoulders back.
- Hold the object as close to your body as possible.
- Lift to a height where you can easily see what's around you. **NEVER** lift an object above shoulder level.

**THE RIGHT WAY! THE WRONG WAY!**

---

**B** Read the safety notice again. Read the statements. Circle *True* or *False*. Correct the false statements.

| | | | |
|---|---|---|---|
| 1. | Before you lift an object, you should look at it carefully. | True | False |
| 2. | If you can push an object, you can lift it. | True | False |
| 3. | Your feet should be as far apart as your hips. | True | False |
| 4. | You should never bend your legs when lifting. | True | False |
| 5. | It's important to use your back muscles when lifting an object. | True | False |
| 6. | You should not twist your body as you lift. | True | False |
| 7. | Hold the object you are lifting away from your body. | True | False |
| 8. | Never lift an object above eye level. | True | False |

## PRACTICAL LISTENING

**A** ◀))) Susan is attending a meeting on workplace safety. Listen to the lecture. What safety topic is the speaker discussing?

**B** ◀))) Listen to the safety lecture again. Then read the questions and complete the answers.

1. What are the causes of slips, trips, and falls in the workplace?

   a. _____ floors, from being cleaned or from something that spilled

   b. floors that are _____ or rugs that are _____

   c. _____ around the building in bad weather

   d. wearing the wrong kind of _____

2. What are some ways to prevent slips, trips, and falls in the workplace?

   a. Make sure floors are _____ and in good _____.

   b. Be sure floors are _____ when possible.

   c. When floors are being cleaned, the area should be _____.

   d. Employees should always wear _____.

   e. When employees see unsafe conditions, they should _____ _____.

## WHAT DO YOU THINK?

**GROUPS OF 3** Describe some of the safety issues in your workplace. Do you think that your employer provides enough training to prevent workplace injuries? Explain your answer.

### 4

## Report an accident

### GET READY TO WATCH

Susan saw an accident between a food service worker and an intern. Have you ever witnessed an accident at work? What happened?

### WATCH

**A**  ◼◀ **Watch the video. What happened when Tom was serving lunch?**

**B**  ◼◀ **Watch the video again. Read the statements. Circle *True* or *False*. Correct the false statements.**

| | | |
|---|---|---|
| 1. The food service worker ran into an intern. | True | False |
| 2. The intern broke a safety rule. | True | False |
| 3. The intern helped clean up the mess. | True | False |
| 4. The food service worker stayed with Mr. Sánchez until a new tray of food came. | True | False |

### CONVERSATION

**A**  ◼◀ **Watch part of the video. Complete the conversation.**

**Susan:** Sorry I'm late, Henry. There was a little accident.

**Henry:** Uh-oh. What happened?

**Susan:** Well, Tom was serving _____.
He was just about to go in to
Mr. Sánchez's room . . .

**Henry:** OK . . .

**Susan:** And Mark, the new intern, was walking the other way and just ran right into him.

**Henry:** Oh, no! Was anybody _____?

**Susan:** No. Luckily everyone was fine.

> **Pronunciation Note**
>
> We use stress and intonation to show the most important word in a sentence.
>
> ◀)) **Listen and repeat.**
>
> There was a little **ac**cident.
>
> Tom was pretty up**set** about it.

**B**  ◀)) **Listen and repeat.**

**C**  PAIRS **Practice the conversation.**

**D**  PAIRS **Make similar conversations.
Talk about an accident you have seen.**

### WHAT DO YOU THINK?

GROUPS OF 3 If someone causes an accident to happen to you, it's natural to feel angry about it. What is the best way to deal with this in the workplace?

# GRAMMAR

**5**

## Past continuous

 **STUDY  Past continuous**

**Statements**

| Subject | was/were (not) | Verb + -ing | |
|---|---|---|---|
| He | was | getting | the tray. |
| We | were not | walking | down the hall. |

**Grammar Note**

Use the past continuous for actions that were in progress at a specific time in the past.

**Yes/No Questions**

| Was/Were | Subject | Verb + -ing | | Short Answers |
|---|---|---|---|---|
| Was | she | helping | Mr. Sánchez? | Yes, she was. / No, she wasn't. |
| Were | you | talking | on the phone? | Yes, I was. / No, I wasn't. |

See page 158 for a review of the past forms of the verb *be*.
See page 158 for a review of spelling rules for continuous forms.

## PRACTICE

**A** **Circle the correct past continuous form.**

1. A nurse (was) / were walking down the hall and slipped.

2. The janitor was / were mopping the floor, so it was wet.

3. Was / Were you waiting for a phone call earlier?

4. The workers wasn't / weren't eating their lunch at the usual time.

5. I was / were hoping to make an appointment for today, but I couldn't.

6. We wasn't / weren't expecting you to be here so soon.

7. Was / Were Frank organizing the stock room this morning?

**B** **Complete the conversations with the correct past continuous form of the verbs.**

1. **Nurse 1:** _____*Was*_____ the aide _____*talking*_____ on her phone?
   <br>                                                     talk

   **Nurse 2:** No, she _____. She _____ a message.
   <br>                                                                            send

2. **Susan:** I _____ my rounds and saw the accident.
   <br>                                    finish

   **Henry:** _____ you _____ to visit Mr. Sánchez?
   <br>                                                              plan

   **Susan:** No, I _____.

3. **Orderly:** _____ the patients _____ for the nurse?
   <br>                                                                  wait

   **Manager:** Yes, they _____. But they _____ for very long.
   <br>                                                                                  not / wait

**C** **Then practice the conversations.**

## WHAT ABOUT YOU?

**PAIRS** What were you doing yesterday at noon? at 4 P.M.? at 8 P.M.? Tell your partner.

## GET READY

Susan is reading an article about distracted walking. Do you walk
and use a cell phone to talk or text at the same time?

### Reading Skill

When you **scan for details** in a reading, you are looking for specific
pieces of information. You move your eyes quickly over the text to
find the details you need.

**Read the Reading Skill. Scan the article. Find and underline:**

**1.** an example of an accident that happened.

**2.** the number of accidents involving mobile electronics that happened in 2011.

**3.** an example of an action that cities are taking because of the accidents.

## READ

◀)) **Listen and read the article. What can happen when people
do not pay attention as they walk and use an electronic device?**

# Talk, Text, Crash!

You've probably seen the videos on the
Internet. A woman accidentally walks into a
water fountain while shopping at the mall.
A man strolls right up to a wild bear in his
backyard, not even realizing it's there. A teen
doesn't notice an open manhole cover
and falls into a smelly sewer. What
do all of these incidents have in
common? The people were all
texting while walking.
Fortunately, these three didn't
get hurt. But accidents like these
are becoming more common.
And some result in more than
just a hilarious video.

In the U.S., a pedestrian is struck
and injured by a car every eight
minutes. In 2011, there were over 1,150
accidents involving mobile electronics.[1] That's
an increase of 400% in the last seven years.
Many of these accidents caused serious injury
and even death.

Many cities are taking action to stop distracted
walking accidents. People who walk and text in
Fort Lee, New Jersey, can earn an $85 fine.
Other cities have started information
campaigns to warn people of the dangers. On
busy streets in Wilmington, Delaware, there
are signs reminding walkers to "Look up!"

Philadelphia tried a humorous approach.
They painted a fake "e-lane" on a
downtown sidewalk. Signs said the
lane was for "citizens with busy
lives who don't have time to look
up from their electronic devices."
Unfortunately, some people
didn't get the joke. They thought
it was a great idea!

Reactions to the laws are mixed.
"I think these fines are a good idea,
especially if they save lives," says
Robert Green. "People need to learn to pay
attention." Julie Adams disagrees: "We need to
rethink these laws. Do we really need the
government to tell us where we can use our
phones? You can't force people to have
common sense!"

[1] Source: Consumer Product Safety Commission

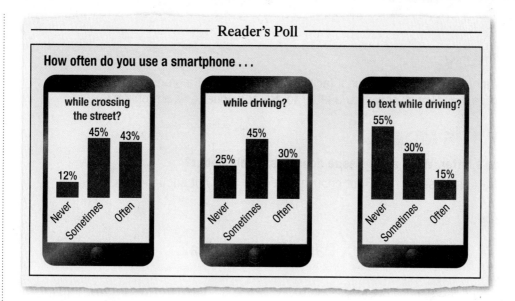

Reader's Poll

How often do you use a smartphone . . .

while crossing the street?
- Never 12%
- Sometimes 45%
- Often 43%

while driving?
- Never 25%
- Sometimes 45%
- Often 30%

to text while driving?
- Never 55%
- Sometimes 30%
- Often 15%

## AFTER YOU READ

**Look at the graph about cell phone use. Answer the questions.**

**1.** What percentage of people never use a cell phone when crossing the street? _____

**2.** What percentage of people often send text messages while driving? _____

**3.** Which activity do 30% of the people admit to doing often? _____

## VOCABULARY STUDY  Prefixes

**Build Your Vocabulary**

A **prefix** is a letter or a group of letters that you add to the beginning of a word in order to make a new word. For example, if you add the prefix "un" to the word *happy*, you get the word *unhappy*.

| Prefix | Meaning | Example |
|--------|---------|---------|
| un- | not, or the opposite of | unwell (not well), untie (to open something that is tied) |
| re- | again | review (to study something again) |
| dis- | not | disadvantage (a bad feature of something) |

**Read the Build Your Vocabulary note. Study the prefixes and their meanings. Then add prefixes to the words below to make new words from the article. The meaning of each new word will match the definition on the right.**

**1.** _____ think: to think again about something

**2.** _____ agree: not agree

**3.** _____ fortunate: something that is not good

> **ON THE WEB**
>
> For more information, go online and search "distracted walking." Look for distracted walking news and report back to the class.

## WHAT DO YOU THINK?

**GROUPS OF 3** Do you think cities should pass laws to prevent accidents caused by distracted walking? How can the government educate people about the problem?

## Write a letter of opinion

### GET READY

Susan is writing a letter to the hospital facilities manager about a problem in the hospital parking garage. Have you ever written a letter to ask someone to fix a problem?

### STUDY THE MODEL

**A** **Read Susan's letter. What safety issue does Susan talk about?**

☐ the elevator isn't safe     ☐ not enough lighting     ☐ not enough exits

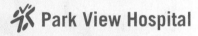
**Park View Hospital**

May 10, 2015

Dear Mr. Peters:

I am an LVN here at Park View. I'm writing to you because I am concerned about a safety issue.

Sometimes I work the evening shift, and when I go home, it is dark. In my opinion, the parking garage does not have enough lighting. I don't always feel safe there. I think that we need better lighting. In particular, I believe we need more lighting near the elevators and at the exits and entrances. There are enough lights above the cars. However, they are not very bright. Therefore, I think these should be replaced with brighter lights.

I really feel that the hospital should install better lighting before winter, when it gets dark earlier. Better lighting will help make a lot of workers like me feel safer.

Thanks very much for considering this.

Sincerely,

*Susan Kim*

Susan Kim

> **Writing Tip**
>
> When you write, it is important to connect your ideas. This helps readers move easily from one thought to another. Use **transition words** such as *also*, *therefore*, and *however* to show the relationship between ideas.

**B** **Read the Writing Tip. Then read Susan's letter again. Underline the transition words.**

**C** Look at and complete the chart Susan used to plan her writing.

| Objective: To have better lighting installed in the parking garage. | |
| --- | --- |
| **What am I asking for?** | better lighting—brighter lights, or more lights |
| **Where do we need this?** | in the _____ |
| **Why do we need this?** | workers leaving at night do not feel safe |
| **When do we need this?** | before _____, when it gets dark earlier |
| **More information** | We need more lighting in the elevator area and the garage. Lighting above the cars should be _____. |

## BEFORE YOU WRITE

**A** PAIRS How can your workplace or school be improved so that it is safer or more convenient? List five ideas.

1. _____

2. _____

3. _____

4. _____

5. _____

**B** You're going to write a letter of opinion to a supervisor or school administrator. Choose one of the ideas from your list. Create a chart to plan your letter.

| Objective: | |
| --- | --- |
| **What am I asking for?** | |
| **Where do we need this?** | |
| **Why do we need this?** | |
| **When do we need this?** | |
| **More information** | |

## WRITE

Review the model and the Writing Tip. Use the ideas from your chart to write your letter.

## 8    Ask for and give clarification

 **GET READY TO WATCH**

Susan is giving instructions to Mr. Galvis but he doesn't understand something she just said. When you don't understand someone, or don't hear them well, what are some things you can say?

 **WATCH**

 **Watch the video. Answer the questions. Circle the correct answers.**

1. When will Mr. Galvis's father probably be going home?
   **a.** today          **b.** tomorrow          **c.** in a week

2. How often should Mr. Galvis's father change his bandage?
   **a.** every day          **b.** every other day          **c.** every three days

3. What else does Susan say Mr. Galvis's father should do?
   **a.** get more exercise          **b.** take some medicine          **c.** stretch his ankle

 **CONVERSATION**

**A**    **Watch part of the video. Complete the conversation.**

**Mr. Galvis:**   Do you know when my dad will be ready to come home?

**Susan:**   He may be ready by tomorrow. The doctor will take a look at his ankle in the morning, and then she'll _____.

**Mr. Galvis:**   OK. Thank you. And is there anything I should know? I mean, about his care?

**Susan:**   Well, he should _____ his bandage every other day.

**Mr. Galvis:**   I'm sorry. I didn't catch that. Did you say, "every day"?

**Susan:**   No, every other day. But he can change it more often if it's bothering him.

**Mr. Galvis:**   All right, I understand.

**B**   ◀))) **Listen and repeat.**

**C**   PAIRS **Practice the conversation.**

**D**   PAIRS **Make similar conversations.**
**Give other instructions for the patient's care.**

| Instructions for the patient |
| --- |
| • take medicine twice a day |
| • change the bandage every morning |
| • get plenty of rest |
| • (your own idea) |

**WHAT DO YOU THINK?**

GROUPS OF 3 Mr. Galvis is planning to help his father at home. How much responsibility do you think children have for taking care of their elderly parents? What are some of the challenges in doing this?

# JOB-SEEKING SKILLS
## Read a job ad

## GET READY

Mario is looking at job ads on the Park View Hospital website. Have you ever looked at job ads online? What kind of information do they usually have?

## READ A JOB AD

**A**  **Read the job ad. What position is the ad for?**

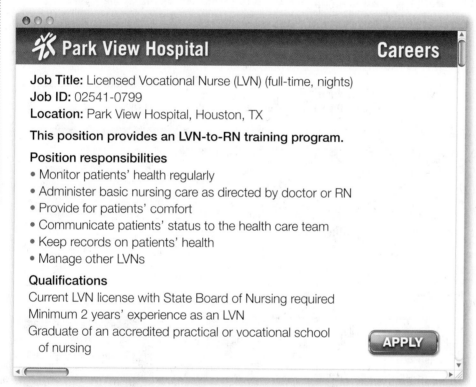

**Park View Hospital**    **Careers**

**Job Title:** Licensed Vocational Nurse (LVN) (full-time, nights)
**Job ID:** 02541-0799
**Location:** Park View Hospital, Houston, TX

**This position provides an LVN-to-RN training program.**

**Position responsibilities**
- Monitor patients' health regularly
- Administer basic nursing care as directed by doctor or RN
- Provide for patients' comfort
- Communicate patients' status to the health care team
- Keep records on patients' health
- Manage other LVNs

**Qualifications**
Current LVN license with State Board of Nursing required
Minimum 2 years' experience as an LVN
Graduate of an accredited practical or vocational school of nursing

**APPLY**

**B**  **Read the job ad again. Mark each statement *True* or *False*. Correct the false statements.**

| | | |
|---|---|---|
| **1.** This LVN position is full-time. | True | False |
| **2.** The position is for the day shift. | True | False |
| **3.** With this LVN position you will manage other nurses. | True | False |
| **4.** You must have worked as an LVN for 3 years to apply for this position. | True | False |
| **5.** You must have an RN license to apply for this position. | True | False |

## PUT YOUR IDEAS TO WORK

**A**  **PAIRS Talk about your dream job. What responsibilities will you have? What qualification will you need to get the job?**

**B**  **Imagine your perfect job. Write an ad for that job on a separate piece of paper.**

## GRAMMAR

In this unit, you studied:

- *Used to*
- Past continuous

See page 147 for your Grammar Review.

## VOCABULARY See page 163 for the Unit 3 Vocabulary.

**Vocabulary Learning Strategy: Learn Words That Go Together**

**A** Find words from the Unit 3 Word List that are used together.
Complete the missing words.

| | | |
|---|---|---|
| _____ a baby | keep someone _____ | a nervous _____ |
| _____ sense | every other _____ | a medical _____ |
| go over _____ | just in _____ | go over _____ |

**B** Circle five groups of words that are used together in Exercise A.
Write a sentence with each one.

## SPELLING See page 163 for the Unit 3 Vocabulary.

**CLASS** Choose ten words for a spelling test.

## LISTENING PLUS

**A** Watch each video. Write the story of Susan's day.

> Susan talked to the grandmother of a patient. The woman told Susan about
> how things were different when she was younger.

**B** **PAIRS** Review the Lesson 4 conversation. See page 38. Role play the conversation
for the class.

## NOW I CAN

**PAIRS** See page 33 for the Unit 3 Goals. Check ☑ the things you can do.
Underline the things you want to study more. Tell your partner.

> I can _____. I need more practice with _____.

# 4 Henry's Big Dreams

## MY GOALS

- [ ] Talk about a job I want
- [ ] Talk about my work history
- [ ] Read a pay stub
- [ ] Offer to help someone
- [ ] Complete a job application

Go to MyEnglishLab for more practice after each lesson.

**Henry Keita**

**Henry**  *Today*
I'm the head nurse in the OR. I like what I do, but maybe it's time to try something new.

47

## 1

## Talk about a job you want

### GET READY TO WATCH

Henry is telling Rick about a job he wants. What is your dream job? How long have you wanted to have that job?

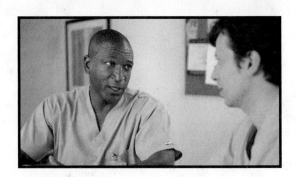

### WATCH

**▶◀ Watch the video. Read the statements. Circle True or False. Correct the false statements.**

| | | | |
|---|---|---|---|
| **1.** | Rick doesn't like his job. | True | False |
| **2.** | Henry works in the Emergency Room. | True | False |
| **3.** | Henry wants a job where he can be helpful. | True | False |
| **4.** | Henry wants a job that isn't very fast-paced. | True | False |

### CONVERSATION

**A** **▶◀ Watch part of the video. Complete the conversation.**

**Henry:** You know, I've always wanted to work in an ER.

**Rick:** Really?

**Henry:** Yeah. I like the idea of _____ the people who need it the most.

**Rick:** It's definitely rewarding.

**Henry:** And I think I'd like to try a more fast-paced job.

**Rick:** This is about as fast-paced as they get. But you're in the OR, right?

Don't you like _____ there?

**Henry:** I do. But I think I can do more.

**B** ◀)) Listen and repeat.

**C** PAIRS Practice the conversation.

**D** PAIRS Talk about a job you want. Give three reasons why you want it. Explain why you would be good at that job.

**E** PAIRS Make similar conversations. Use your ideas from Exercise D.

## WHAT DO YOU THINK?

**GROUPS OF 3** If you have a good job, is it a good idea to change to another job? Why or why not?

# GRAMMAR

## Present perfect: Indefinite past

## STUDY Present perfect

### Statements

| Subject | *have* (*not*) | Past Participle | |
|---|---|---|---|
| I | have not | worked | in the ER. |

### Statements with Adverbs

| Subject | *have* (*not*) | Adverb | Past Participle | |
|---|---|---|---|---|
| I | have not | always | wanted | a fast-paced job. |
| Henry | has | never | had | the chance. |

### Yes/No Questions

| *Have* | Subject | (*ever*) | Past Participle | |
|---|---|---|---|---|
| Have | you | ever | asked | for a transfer? |

### Short Answers

| |
|---|
| Yes, I have. / No, I haven't. |
| Yes, she has. / No, she hasn't. |

### Grammar Note

Use the present perfect to talk about things that happened at an indefinite time in the past.
Use the simple past if the time is mentioned.

See page 159 for a list of past participle forms for common irregular verbs.

## PRACTICE

**A** **Circle the simple past or the present perfect form.**

**1.** Henry (got) / has gotten his Associate's degree in 1999.

**2.** He became / has become a staff nurse in 2000.

**3.** Has Henry always work / worked as a nurse at Park View Hospital?

**4.** I thought / have thought about changing jobs last year, but I changed my mind.

**B** **Complete the conversations with the present perfect and the correct form of the verb.**

**1. A:** I ___'ve___ always ___dreamed___ of becoming an engineer.
          (dream)

   **B:** _____ you _____ going to school for that?
                      (consider)

**2. A:** _____ you ever _____ about changing careers?
                              (think)

   **B:** Yes, I _____. But I'm not sure it's a good idea.

**3. A:** _____ Angela always _____ a waitress?
                                    (be)

   **B:** No. She _____ also _____ as a dishwasher.
                                      (work)

## WHAT ABOUT YOU?

**PAIRS** What jobs have you had that you enjoyed? What jobs would you like to do?

# 3 Use supporting illustrations

## GET READY

**A** Henry read an online article about strange jobs. Have you heard about a strange or unusual job?

**B** Read the Reading Skill. Look at the illustrations in the article. Can you guess what each person is doing?

## READ

◀))) Listen and read the article. Was your guess correct?

**Reading Skill**

**Supporting illustrations** are art or photos that are included with an article. Writers use illustrations to help the reader understand the meaning of the text. Look at the illustrations of a text before you read to get an idea of what the article is about.

### So What Do *You* Do For A Living?

"I never thought I'd be doing this," Joe Merone says about his strange career as a cook. What's unusual about being a cook? Joe is a Culinary Specialist on a nuclear submarine. "I was working in a restaurant and met a customer from the navy. He said that if I wanted a challenge, I should try cooking underwater," explains Joe. "I wanted something new, so I enlisted. I've learned a lot. We run out of fresh ingredients after a few weeks at sea, so I've really learned how to get the most out of canned food. I just had to get used to not having any windows!"

Like Joe, many people find themselves working jobs they never even knew existed. Here are a few more unusual careers that may surprise you.

**Foley Artist** Did you know that most sounds in a movie are not made by the actors? Studios later add background noises, such as footsteps. Sound experts, called Foley artists, find creative ways to make any sound the studio may need. For example, they may shake a sheet of metal to simulate thunder or slap gloves together for flapping bird wings. **Average salary: $80,000.**

**Golf Ball Diver** Ever wonder what happens to balls that land in the water on golf courses? They're collected by professional golf ball divers wearing SCUBA gear. A good diver can recover 1,000 balls an hour, earning about $100. If that sounds like easy work, think again. The divers feel for balls with their hands in total darkness. They often get cut by broken glass and bitten by snakes! **Average salary: $35,000.**

**Breath Odor Tester** How do mouthwash companies know that their products stop bad breath? They employ people with an excellent sense of smell to test them! These fearless workers smell people's breath before and after they use the mouthwash. Then they evaluate how well it works. **Average salary: $53,000.**

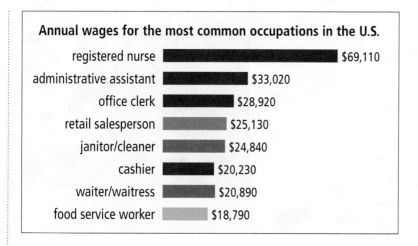

**Annual wages for the most common occupations in the U.S.**

| Occupation | Annual Wage |
|---|---|
| registered nurse | $69,110 |
| administrative assistant | $33,020 |
| office clerk | $28,920 |
| retail salesperson | $25,130 |
| janitor/cleaner | $24,840 |
| cashier | $20,230 |
| waiter/waitress | $20,890 |
| food service worker | $18,790 |

## AFTER YOU READ

**Look at the graph about average annual job salaries. Answer the questions.**

1. What is the average annual pay for a waiter? _____

2. Which job earns an average annual wage of $24,840? _____

3. Which job has the highest pay? _____

## VOCABULARY STUDY  Suffixes

**Build Your Vocabulary**

A **suffix** is a group of letters that you add to the end of a word to make a new word. For example, you add *-dom* to *king* to make *kingdom*, the land of a king.

| Suffix | Meaning | Examples |
|---|---|---|
| **-er / -or** | a person or thing who | teacher, player, actor, calculator |
| **-ness** | the condition of, full of | quietness, kindness, sadness |
| **-less** | without | careless, sleepless, priceless |

**Read the Build Your Vocabulary note. Study the suffixes and their meanings. Then complete the definitions of words from the article.**

1. A *diver* is a person who _____.

2. *Darkness* means the condition of being _____.

3. A *tester* is a person who _____.

4. *Fearless* means without _____.

## WHAT DO YOU THINK?

**GROUPS OF 3** What are some good and bad features of the unusual jobs mentioned in the article? Would you like to have one of these jobs? Why or why not?

**ON THE WEB**

For more information, go online and search "strange jobs." Find a strange job and tell the class about it.

## 4 Talk about your work history

### GET READY TO WATCH

Rick is telling Henry about his work history. What was your first job? Is it related to what you are doing now? Is it related to your dream job?

### WATCH

 **Watch the video. Circle the correct words.**

1. Rick has experience working with children / the elderly.

2. Rick has / doesn't have any regrets about his current job.

3. Rick thinks that OR / ER work is intense.

### CONVERSATION

**A**  **Watch part of the video. Complete the conversation.**

**Henry:** So, have you always been an ER _____?

**Rick:** Oh, no. I started out in outpatient care.

**Henry:** No kidding.

**Rick:** Yeah. I was mostly helping elderly _____.
I liked that a lot.

**Henry:** Then why did you change jobs?

**Rick:** The hospital needed ER nurses. It seemed like

a good _____ opportunity.

**Henry:** So you got your training.

**Rick:** Right. And I've been here since then.

**B** 🔊 **Listen and repeat.**

**C** PAIRS **Practice the conversation.**

**D** PAIRS **Make similar conversations. Talk about your current job and your own work history.**

> **Pronunciation Note**
>
> When we say an abbreviation using the letters of the alphabet, we usually stress the last letter.
>
> 🔊 **Listen and repeat.**
>
> an ER nurse      the OR      on TV

### WHAT DO YOU THINK?

**GROUPS OF 3** In the video, Henry says, "The grass is always greener on the other side of the fence." What do you think he means by this? Do you think this expression is true?

# Present perfect with *for* and *since*

## STUDY  Present perfect with *for* and *since*

**Statements**

| Subject | *have* | Past Participle | | *for/since* | Time Expression |
|---|---|---|---|---|---|
| I | have | worked | here | for | ten years. |
| He | has | been | a nurse | since | 2005. |

**Wh- Questions**

| Wh- Word | *have* | Subject | Past Participle | |
|---|---|---|---|---|
| How long | have | you | worked | here? |

**Short Answers**

| |
|---|
| (**For**) ten years. |
| **Since** 2013. |

**Grammar Note**

Use the present perfect with *for* or *since* to talk about something that started in the past and is still true.
Use *for* with a length of time (*for ten minutes, for a month, for a long time*).
Use *since* with a specific time (*since 5:00, since Monday, since two days ago*).

## PRACTICE

**A**  Circle *for* or *since*.

1. Michel has worked as a receptionist here (**for**) / since three years.

2. Charlie has been an LPN for / since last year.

3. Has Sheila been the head nurse for / since a long time?

4. I have waited tables at this restaurant for / since five months.

5. We've worked together for / since January.

**B**  Look at the timeline. On a separate piece of paper, write 5 sentences about Henry. Use the present perfect with *for* or *since*.

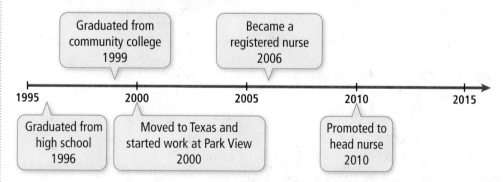

| Graduated from community college 1999 | | Became a registered nurse 2006 |

1995 — 2000 — 2005 — 2010 — 2015

| Graduated from high school 1996 | Moved to Texas and started work at Park View 2000 | Promoted to head nurse 2010 |

**C**  PAIRS  Ask and answer questions with *How long* about Henry.

## WHAT ABOUT YOU?

Create a timeline for important events in your life. With a partner, ask and answer questions with *How long*.

## GET READY

Henry has just received his pay stub, and he is checking it for errors.
Do you check pay stubs for mistakes?

## PRACTICAL READING

**A** **Read the pay stub. What kinds of information do you see?**
**Check [✓] all that are correct.**

☐  how many hours Henry worked

☐  how much money Henry earned per hour

☐  how much tax has been taken away

☐  how much Henry paid for health insurance

☐  how many times Henry was late to work

### Park View Hospital

**Name:** Henry Keita
**Employee ID #** 409-773-821
**Base Rate:** 30.26

**Pay Date:** 5/17
**Pay Period:** 5/1 – 5/15

| Hours and Earnings | | | Taxes and Deductions | | Pre-Tax Items | |
|---|---|---|---|---|---|---|
| Regular | 80 | 2420.80 | FICA | 202.19 | Health | 104.84 |
| Overtime | 10 | 453.90 | Fed Inc Tax | 740.04 | Dental | 40.63 |
| | | | | | 401K | 86.24 |

| | Gross | Pre-Tax | Taxable Wages | Taxes and Deductions | Net Pay |
|---|---|---|---|---|---|
| Current | 2874.70 | 231.71 | 2642.99 | 942.23 | 1700.76 |
| YTD | 25191.45 | 2064.97 | 23126.48 | 8244.59 | 14881.89 |

**B** **Read the pay stub again. Answer the questions. Circle the the correct answers.**

**1.** When did this pay period begin?

   **a.** May 1      **b.** May 15      **c.** May 17

**2.** How long is this pay period?

   **a.** 1 week      **b.** 2 weeks      **c.** 1 month

**3.** How many regular hours does Henry work per week?

   **a.** 10 hours      **b.** 40 hours      **c.** 80 hours

**4.** How many overtime hours did Henry work in this pay period?

   **a.** 80 hours      **b.** 30.26 hours      **c.** 10 hours

**5.** Which of these items is not taxed?

   **a.** overtime hours      **b.** regular hours      **c.** 401K contribution

**C** Answer the questions. Write the correct amount from the pay stub.

1. How much money does Henry earn for a regular hour of work? _____

2. How much money did Henry make this pay period before taxes? _____

3. How much of this amount will be taxed? _____

4. How much tax does Henry have to pay for this pay period? _____

5. What is Henry's net pay for this pay period? _____

6. What is Henry's net pay from January 1 to May 15? _____

## PRACTICAL SPEAKING

**A** ◀)) **An employee has a question about his pay stub. He talks to his human resources manager. Listen to their conversation.**

**Employee:** Excuse me. Do you have a minute?

**Manager:** Sure. What is it?

**Employee:** I have a question about my paycheck.

**Manager:** OK. Let's take a look. What is it?

**Employee:** Can you explain to me what "FICA" is?

**Manager:** That's a tax you pay the government for Social Security and Medicare.

**Employee:** Oh, I see. Thanks!

**B** ◀)) **Listen and repeat.**

**C** **PAIRS** Role play a conversation between an employee and a human resources manager. Ask about different items on a pay stub.

## PRACTICAL LISTENING

**A** ◀)) **Henry is listening to a podcast about double-checking your pay stub. Listen to the podcast. Which item on the pay stub is the audio *mostly* about?**

a. gross and net pay     b. FICA     c. overtime hours

**B** ◀)) **Listen again. Read the statements. Circle *True* or *False*. Correct the false statements.**

| | | |
|---|---|---|
| 1. You can choose not to have FICA taxes taken away from your paycheck. | True | False |
| 2. Social Security and Medicare benefits are based on the number of years you have been retired. | True | False |
| 3. If your employer makes a mistake, you might receive less money after retirement. | True | False |
| 4. The amount of FICA withholding should be 7.65% of your net pay. | True | False |
| 5. If you see a mistake, you should talk to a coworker about it. | True | False |

## WHAT DO YOU THINK?

**GROUPS OF 3** Why do you think it is important to save your pay stubs? For how long should you save them?

## Write a short biography

**GET READY**

Henry read about a new employee in the hospital newsletter. When you meet people for the first time, what things do you like to learn about them?

**STUDY THE MODEL**

**A** Read the biography. Which paragraph talks about Cam's previous work experience?

### Meet Cam Trung
**Administrative Coordinator, Nursing Department**

1 We are happy to welcome Cam Trung to Park View Hospital. Cam joined the administrative team in the nursing department last month.

2 Before coming to Park View, Cam worked at the West Side Medical Clinic as an administrative support person. At West Side, Cam was part of a team that created a new system for storing patient information.

3 Cam has known since high school that she wanted to work in a hospital. "I've always been interested in health care," she says. "When I was a teenager I volunteered at my local hospital and at a nursing home. I loved helping people." Cam is thrilled with the opportunity to join us at Park View. "I'm excited to be a part of the team. Everyone has been very friendly, and I'm already learning a lot of new skills."

4 In her free time, Cam loves to cook. On weekends, she often invites friends over for barbeques and games of basketball. Cam lives in Bellaire with her husband Danh and five-year-old son Chad.

5 Cam works in the nursing department office on the fourth floor. Be sure to stop by and say hello!

> **Writing Tip**
>
> When you write a text that has more than one paragraph, each paragraph should have just one **main idea**. The main idea tells you the most important information in the paragraph. Usually, this main idea is in the first or second sentence of each paragraph.

**B** Read the Writing Tip. Then read the biography again.
Match each paragraph to its main idea.

_____ Paragraph 1     **a.** work history

_____ Paragraph 2     **b.** personal interests

_____ Paragraph 3     **c.** introduction to Cam

_____ Paragraph 4     **d.** where to meet Cam

_____ Paragraph 5     **e.** motivation for career

**C** Look at and complete the ideas web the author used to plan the biography.

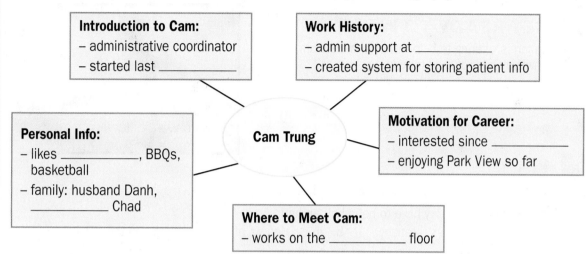

**Introduction to Cam:**
– administrative coordinator
– started last _____

**Work History:**
– admin support at _____
– created system for storing patient info

**Personal Info:**
– likes _____, BBQs, basketball
– family: husband Danh, _____ Chad

**Cam Trung**

**Motivation for Career:**
– interested since _____
– enjoying Park View so far

**Where to Meet Cam:**
– works on the _____ floor

## BEFORE YOU WRITE

**A** **PAIRS** You're going to write a biography of your partner. Interview your partner. Ask the questions below. Add two of your own questions.

**1.** What is your name? _____

**2.** Do you live with family members? Who? _____
_____

**3.** What do you do? Where do you work? What do you do there? _____
_____

**4.** What other English classes have you taken, before this one? _____
_____

**5.** Why are you studying English? What are your goals? _____
_____

**6.** What do you like to do in your free time? _____
_____

**7.** Your question: _____
Answer: _____

**8.** Your question: _____
Answer: _____

**B** Create an ideas web using the answers your partner gave you in Exercise A. Use a separate piece of paper.

## WRITE

Write a biography about your partner from Exercise A. Review the model and the Writing Tip. Use the ideas from your ideas web to write your biography.

## 8  Offer to help someone

### GET READY TO WATCH

Susan is offering to help Henry with his work.
Have you ever offered to help a coworker?

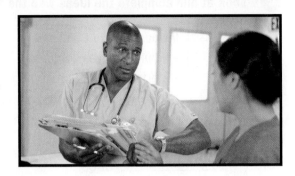

### WATCH

◼◀ **Watch the video. Circle the correct answers.**

1. Where does Henry have to be in half an hour?
   a. at the nurses' station    b. in Dr. Healy's office    c. in the OR

2. What does Henry ask Susan to do with the file?
   a. bring a copy to a doctor    b. make some notes in it    c. copy it for herself

3. What does Susan think Henry should do?
   a. make his own copies    b. ask for help more often    c. help the other nurses

### CONVERSATION

**A**  ◼◀ **Watch part of the video. Complete the conversation.**

**Henry:** I'm so busy. And I'm due in the OR in half an hour.

**Susan:** Can I help with anything?

**Henry:** Actually, yeah. I could really use some help.

**Susan:** Of course. Just tell me what you need me to do.

**Henry:** Well, I need to make a _____ of this file.
Then I have to bring it up to Dr. Healy on the fourth floor.

**Susan:** OK. I'll take care of it. And I should bring the original back to you, right?

**Henry:** Yes, that's right. Thanks a lot.
That's a big _____.

**Susan:** No problem. Anytime.

**B**  ◀)) **Listen and repeat.**

**C**  **PAIRS Practice the conversation.**

**D**  **PAIRS Make similar conversations.**
**Offer to help someone with a task.**

> **Pronunciation Note**
>
> Some words have letters that we do not pronounce.
>
> ◀)) **Listen and repeat. Notice the silent letters.**
>
> | half | hour | could |
> |------|------|-------|
> | should | right | often |

### WHAT DO YOU THINK?

**GROUPS OF 3** Do you think Susan gave Henry good advice?
Is it OK for her to give this kind of advice to a supervisor?

# JOB-SEEKING SKILLS

## Complete a job application

**Mario López** *Today*
Frank told me that Park View Hospital is looking for nurses! I'm going to fill out an application right away!

## GET READY

Mario is completing a job application for the LVN position at Park View Hospital. Have you ever filled out a job application? What job was the application for?

## READD A JOB APPLICATION

**A** **Read the job application. What information does it ask for?**

### ✳ Park View Hospital  1550 Park Rd., Houston, TX 77004

| Last Name | First Name | Middle Name | Telephone Number |
|---|---|---|---|
| LÓPEZ | MARIO | LUIS | Home (281) 555-7812    Cell (832) 555-0329 |

| Address | City | State | Zip Code | Date of Application |
|---|---|---|---|---|
| 4180 POLK ST. | HOUSTON | TX | 77023 | 5-17-15 |

| Social Security No. | Drivers License No. | Professional License No./State/Expiration Date |
|---|---|---|
| 000-991-0423 | 58441209 | Lic. No. PN 436 210 / TEXAS / exp. 10-30-17 |

| Education: (Circle Highest Grade Completed) | Name & Address of College, School or Nursing School |
|---|---|
| High School  1  2  3  ④ Yrs<br>College       1  2  3  ④ 5  6  Yrs | MCCLENNAN COMMUNITY COLLEGE,<br>1400 COLLEGE DR., WACO, TX 76708 |

| Position Applying for | Dept. | Starting Salary Expected | Number of Years Experience |
|---|---|---|---|
| LVN | medical / surgical | $43,000 | 5 |

| Are you willing to work on weekends? | What shifts are you willing to work? |
|---|---|
| ⓎYes  No   Will Consider | ⓄDay  ⓄNight  ⓄEvening  Part-Time/Relief  Any |

**B** **Read the job application again. Answer the questions.**

1. What is Mario's professional license number? _____

2. In which city did Mario go to school? _____

3. How long has Mario worked as an LVN? _____

4. Which shifts can Mario work? _____

## PUT YOUR IDEAS TO WORK

**A** **Imagine that you are applying for a job. Complete the application.**

| Education: (Circle Highest Grade Completed) | Name & Address of College, School or Nursing School |
|---|---|
| High School  1  2  3  4  Yrs<br>College       1  2  3  4  5  6  Yrs | |

| Position Applying for | Dept. | Starting Salary Expected | Number of Years Experience |
|---|---|---|---|
| | | | |

| Are you willing to work on weekends? | What shifts are you willing to work? |
|---|---|
| Yes  No   Will Consider | Day  Night  Evening  Part-Time/Relief  Any |

**B** **PAIRS Ask and answer questions about your job applications.**

*What position are you applying for?*

## GRAMMAR

In this unit, you studied:

- Present perfect: Indefinite past
- Present perfect with *for* and *since*

See page 148 for your Grammar Review.

## VOCABULARY  See page 163 for the Unit 4 Vocabulary.

**Vocabulary Learning Strategy: Write Your First Language**

**A** Choose ten words from the Unit 4 Word List. In your notebook, write the word in English and then in your first language.

*stressful—estresante*

**B** Underline five words in Exercise A. Write a sentence with each word.

## SPELLING  See page 163 for the Unit 4 Vocabulary.

**CLASS** Choose ten words for a spelling test.

## LISTENING PLUS

**A** Watch each video. Write the story of Henry's day.

*Henry talked to his coworker Rick about a job he wants. Henry said that he wants to work in an ER.*

**B** **PAIRS** Review the Lesson 8 conversation. See page 58. Role play the conversation for the class.

## NOW I CAN

**PAIRS** See page 47 for the Unit 4 Goals. Check ☑ the things you can do. Underline the things you want to study more. Tell your partner.

I can _____. I need more practice with _____.

# 5 Alina on the Move

## MY GOALS

☐ Talk about exercise habits

☐ Ask for and give advice

☐ Read an apartment rental ad

☐ Ask about an apartment for rent

☐ Complete a job application

Go to MyEnglishLab for more practice after each lesson.

**Alina Morales**

Alina       *Today*
Lots to do at work today! And I need to look for a new apartment after my shift.

61

## 1 Talk about exercise habits

### GET READY TO WATCH

Ida and Alina are planning to take a walk together.
What types of exercise do you enjoy?

### WATCH

■◀ **Watch the video. Complete the sentences.**

1. Ida buys some _____ because she needs some energy.
2. Ida likes to _____ for exercise.
3. Alina likes to _____ for exercise.
4. Alina and Ida will meet later during their _____.

### CONVERSATION

**A** ■◀ **Watch part of the video. Complete the conversation.**

**Alina:** What do you do for exercise?

**Ida:** I like to swim.

**Alina:** Oh, nice. _____ do you do that?

**Ida:** Usually twice a week. What about you?
Do you swim?

**Alina:** No. I'm not much of a swimmer.
I prefer walking.

**Ida:** Oh? Do you walk a lot?

**Alina:** Almost _____.

**Ida:** Wow.

**B** ◀)) **Listen and repeat.**

**C** **PAIRS** **Practice the conversation.**

**D** **PAIRS** **Make similar conversations.**
**Talk about your own exercise habits.**

> **Pronunciation Note**
>
> *Do you* usually has a short, weak
> pronunciation in questions: "d'ya."
> In informal conversation, *What do
> you* often sounds like "Whaddaya."
>
> ◀)) **Listen and repeat.**
>
> **What** do you **do for exercise?**
>
> Do you **walk a lot?**
>
> **When** do you **find time?**

### WHAT DO YOU THINK?

**GROUPS OF 3** Alina and Ida make plans to exercise during their lunch break at work.
What are some other good ways to fit exercise into your schedule?

# GRAMMAR

## 2 Gerunds and infinitives

 **STUDY** Gerunds and infinitives

| Gerunds | | | |
|---|---|---|---|
| Alina | enjoys | **walking**. | |
| Ria | likes | **riding** | her bike. |

| Infinitives | | | |
|---|---|---|---|
| Ida | wants | **to swim** | today. |
| Ria | likes | **to ride** | her bike. |

**Grammar Note**

Use a gerund after the verbs *enjoy*, *don't mind*, *avoid*, *finish*, *feel like*, and *dislike*.
Use an infinitive after the verbs *want*, *need*, *hope*, *plan*, *decide*, and *would like*.
Some common verbs can be followed by either a gerund or an infinitive: *like*,
    *love*, *hate*, *can't stand*, *prefer*, *start*.

See page 160 for more common verbs followed by gerunds and/or infinitives.

## PRACTICE

**A** **Circle the gerund or infinitive form.**

1. Susan avoids to eat / (eating) junk food.

2. Henry doesn't mind to exercise / exercising after his shift.

3. Biata would like to exercise / exercising more every day.

4. Frank plans to lose / losing weight this year.

5. Alina dislikes to go / going to the gym after work.

6. Susan sometimes feels like to have / having a muffin for a snack.

7. Henry enjoys to jog / jogging in his neighborhood.

8. Alina hopes to find / finding fresh vegetables at the market.

**B** **Complete the paragraph with the correct gerund or infinitive form of the verb.**

We need _____ *to protect* _____ our health by eating carefully. Many people enjoy
            1. protect

_____ a little every day. Often they prefer _____ over
        2. exercise                                              3. walk

other exercise. We all want _____ a healthy life. For this, we must decide
                            4. live

_____ regularly. We should also start _____ more fruits
        5. exercise                                         6. eat

and vegetables. I don't mind _____ what I eat. But I never feel like
                            7. watch

_____ when I gain weight!
        8. diet

## WHAT ABOUT YOU?

**PAIRS** Talk about your own health habits. Use verbs from the Grammar Note.

## LESSON **WRITING**

**3** Write about cause and effect

 **GET READY**

Alina's patient needed to change her diet. Alina wrote a report describing the effects of the change. Have you ever decided to change your eating habits?

**STUDY THE MODEL**

 **A** Read the report. What were the results of the patient's change in diet?

---

### ✳ Park View Hospital

**NUTRITION ASSESSMENT AND PLAN OF CARE REPORT**

Patient Name: _Glenda Williams_          Patient ID: _32104_

| Notes: | |
|---|---|
| Dietitian:<br>Alina<br>Morales<br>Date: 5/17/14<br>Time: 2:15 P.M. | I saw this patient for the first time a month ago. She is a little overweight and reported having headaches often. She also complained about feeling tired most of the time. |
| | I diagnosed her as pre-diabetic. I explained that she needs to be careful not to eat too much sugar, because she needs to lower her sugar levels. |
| | Consequently, the patient has changed her diet. She stopped drinking soft drinks and started eating brown rice instead of white rice. She also checks the ingredients on packaged food carefully and pays attention to "hidden sugars." |
| | As a result of these changes, the patient's blood sugar level has gone down. She reports that she gets fewer headaches. She also says that she has more energy and doesn't get tired as quickly. Since she is eating less junk food, she has lost some weight. |

---

**Writing Tip**

When you describe cause and effect, use **transition words**. The transition words *since* and *because* show the cause of something. The transition words *as a result*, *therefore*, and *consequently* show the effect.

**B** Read the Writing Tip. Then read the report again. Underline four cause and effect transition words.

**C** Look at the flow chart Alina used to plan her report, and complete it.

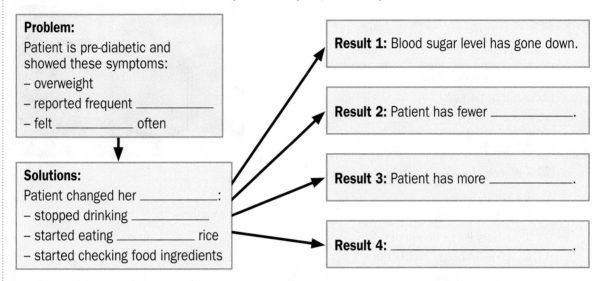

**Problem:**
Patient is pre-diabetic and showed these symptoms:
– overweight
– reported frequent _____
– felt _____ often

**Solutions:**
Patient changed her _____:
– stopped drinking _____
– started eating _____ rice
– started checking food ingredients

**Result 1:** Blood sugar level has gone down.

**Result 2:** Patient has fewer _____.

**Result 3:** Patient has more _____.

**Result 4:** _____.

## BEFORE YOU WRITE

**A** PAIRS Talk about a problem you had. What change did you make to solve the problem? What were the effects of this change?

*I couldn't sleep at night. So I stopped drinking coffee after 2:00 . . .*

**B** You're going to write about the change you discussed in Exercise A.
Create a flow chart to plan your writing. Use a separate piece of paper if necessary.

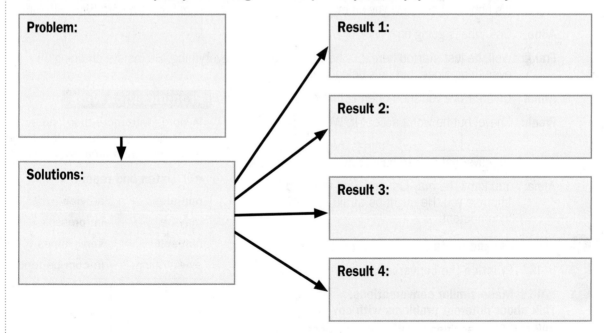

**Problem:**

**Solutions:**

**Result 1:**

**Result 2:**

**Result 3:**

**Result 4:**

## WRITE

Review the model and the Writing Tip. Use the ideas from your flow chart
to write about the change you made and its effects.

 **GET READY TO WATCH**

Frank is asking Alina for advice about a problem at work. When was the last time you asked someone for advice? Who did you ask? Why did you choose that person?

## WATCH

■◀ **Watch the video. Circle the correct answers.**

1. Tal wants to _____.
   a. do everything by himself
   b. get other people to do his work
2. Alina tells Frank he should _____.
   a. give Tal better instructions
   b. praise Tal for things he does well
3. Frank doesn't want to talk to the manager because _____.
   a. Frank doesn't have time to help Tal
   b. Frank doesn't want Tal to get in trouble

## CONVERSATION

(A) ■◀ **Watch part of the video. Complete the conversation.**

**Frank:** Hi, Alina. Do you have a few minutes? I'd like to ask your advice about something.

**Alina:** Of course. What's up?

**Frank:** It's about Tal, the new guy on my _____. I'm having a hard time with him.

**Alina:** Oh? What's going on?

**Frank:** Well, he just started here, but he thinks he knows everything. He insists on doing everything alone, but he's doing it all wrong.

**Alina:** Uh-oh. Have you tried offering him help?

**Frank:** I have, but he won't accept it. When I try to _____ things, he won't listen. He says that he can handle everything himself.

**Alina:** You know, he may just be trying too hard to impress you. He might be afraid of looking incompetent.

(B) ◀)) **Listen and repeat.**

(C) **PAIRS Practice the conversation.**

(D) **PAIRS Make similar conversations. Talk about different problems with coworkers and suggest new ways of dealing with them.**

### Pronunciation Note

In words with more than one syllable, one syllable is stressed. It is longer and louder than other syllables.

◀)) **Listen and repeat.**

| | |
|---|---|
| **min**·utes | ad·**vice** |
| **may**·be | im·**press** |
| him·**self** | **some**·times |
| **ev**·ery·thing | in·**com**·pe·tent |

## WHAT DO YOU THINK?

**GROUPS OF 3** Frank doesn't want to talk to the food services manager about his problem. Do you think he should? Why or why not? What other advice might you give Frank?

# GRAMMAR

## Gerunds after prepositions

### STUDY Gerunds after prepositions

|  | Verb | Preposition | Gerund |  |
|---|---|---|---|---|
| Tal | insists | **on** | **doing** | things alone. |

|  | Adjective | Preposition | Gerund |  |
|---|---|---|---|---|
| Frank is | tired | **of** | **listening** | to him. |

**Grammar Note**

| Adjective + Preposition Combinations | | Verb + Preposition Combinations | |
|---|---|---|---|
| afraid of | interested in | apologize for | look forward to |
| excited about | responsible for | believe in | plan on |
| good at | worried about | complain about | thank (someone) for |

### PRACTICE

**A** Complete the sentences with the correct preposition and the gerund form of the verb.

**1.** Frank is worried ___about working___ with Tal.
<br>　　　　　　　　　　work

**2.** Alina is good _____ with people.
<br>　　　　　　　　deal

**3.** Frank is responsible _____ care of the problem.
<br>　　　　　　　　　　take

**4.** Tal may be afraid _____ a bad job.
<br>　　　　　　　　do

**5.** Everyone is interested _____ a respectful workplace.
<br>　　　　　　　　　have

**6.** Frank is planning _____ with Tal tomorrow.
<br>　　　　　　　speak

**B** Complete the sentences with the correct expressions and the gerund form of the verb.

> believe in　　excited about　　interested in　　~~plan on~~　　responsible for

**1.** I ___plan on joining___ a gym next month. I need to lose some weight.
<br>　　　　　join

**2.** I'd really like a job where I can be _____ my own time.
<br>　　　　　　　　　　　　　　manage

**3.** James is _____ his new job next week. He can't wait!
<br>　　　　　　　start

**4.** I _____ people whenever I can.
<br>　　　　help

**5.** I'm _____ a sport. I'd like to get some exercise.
<br>　　　　play

### WHAT ABOUT YOU?

**GROUPS OF 3** Talk about your plans and fears. Use expressions from the Grammar Note.

*I'm excited about visiting my sister's children next week . . .*

## Understand antecedents

## GET READY

Alina read an online discussion forum for business problems. Have you ever had problems with a coworker? What problems have you had?

☐ Coworker is always late

☐ Coworker doesn't do his or her share of the work

☐ Coworker complains all the time

☐ Other problem: _____

## READ

🔊)) **Listen and read the discussion forum posts. What is Marty Q's problem?**

---

**Working World Wisdom**     Home | All Categories | Business & Finance | Careers & Employment

**Post your work problems and get advice in our discussion forum!**

| Marty Q. | Shirking Coworker | Posted: 5/17/13 6:00 P.M. |
|---|---|---|

How can I deal with a coworker who doesn't do her share of the work? At my job, we work as part of a team. When this person doesn't do her work, the rest of us have to work that much harder. Sometimes we can't finish our work on time, and it makes our team look bad. The problem is as plain as day to all of us, but our manager doesn't seem to know about her shirking yet. What's the right way to handle this?

**Pilarthree:**     Posted: 5/17/13 6:25 P.M.

I had the same problem at my office. Difficult people are everywhere, like ants at a picnic! I'd talk to your manager right away and report what's happening. You don't want to continue working extra hard for this slacker.

[Reply]

**Cableguy22:**     Posted: 5/17/13 7:10 P.M.

I agree with Pilarthree. But I'd add one thing: When you talk to your boss, be sure to explain the situation in an objective way. Stay calm and don't make personal attacks on your coworker. Be cool as a cucumber. Just report the facts. Give examples of things that the person did or didn't do. Let your boss know the negative effect on your team and on the business.

[Reply]

**CarolCatering:**     Posted: 5/17/13 7:33 P.M.

I'm not sure going straight to the boss is a good idea. I supervise 12 employees, and I spend half my time listening to them complain about each other. Nobody likes a whiner! I'll bet your boss already knows about the problem with your coworker. You'll earn your boss's respect by handling the problem yourself.

[Reply]

**Sonia L.:**     Posted: 5/17/13 7:52 P.M.

Have you tried talking to your coworker? It's possible that she doesn't know she's not doing enough. She may not realize the burden she's placing on the other team members. Also, there may be something preventing your coworker from doing her work. Maybe she doesn't know how to do something and is afraid to ask.

[Reply]

---

# AFTER YOU READ

**Reading Skill**

As you read, it is important to recognize **antecedents**. This is the noun that a pronoun replaces in the text. Usually pronouns such as *he*, *she*, *it*, *this*, or *that* come after the noun they replace. By recognizing antecedents, you better follow the sequence and logic of ideas.

**Read the Reading Skill. Read the forum posts again. Then find the sentences below in the forum. In each sentence the pronoun is underlined. Circle the noun (the antecedent) that the pronoun replaces.**

**1.** How can I deal with a coworker who doesn't do her share of the work?

    **a.** the team     **b.** a coworker     **c.** Marty Q.

**2.** What's the right way to handle this?

    **a.** the problem     **b.** the manager     **c.** the team

**3.** I supervise 12 employees, and I spend half my time listening to them complain about each other.

    **a.** the team     **b.** the 12 employees     **c.** the coworker

# VOCABULARY STUDY Similes

**Build Your Vocabulary**

A **simile** compares two very different things. Writers use similes to describe something in an interesting and unexpected way. Similes often use the words *like* or *as*. For example, this sentence contains a simile: *His hands were as cold as ice.*

| Simile | Meaning |
|---|---|
| He's as quiet as a mouse. | He's very quiet. |
| It's as hard as a rock. | It's very hard. |
| She eats like a bird. | She eats very little. |
| Stan ate his soup like a vacuum cleaner. | Stan ate the soup quickly. |

**Read the Build Your Vocabulary note.**
**Then find and complete the similes from the article.**

as plain as _____

like ants _____

as cool as a _____

# WHAT DO YOU THINK?

**GROUPS OF 3** Do you think Marty Q. received good solutions to his problem? Discuss the advantages and disadvantages of each suggestion. What would you do if you were Marty Q.?

**ON THE WEB**

For more information, go online and search "difficult coworkers advice." Find two tips and share with the class.

## GET READY

Alina is looking at apartment rental ads online.
What are some other ways to find apartments?

## PRACTICAL READING

 Read the apartment rental listings. Which apartment has the cheapest monthly rent?

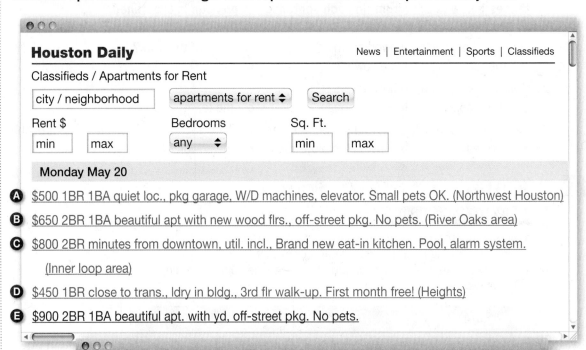

**Houston Daily**     News | Entertainment | Sports | Classifieds

Classifieds / Apartments for Rent

| city / neighborhood | apartments for rent ⇕ | Search |

Rent $         Bedrooms         Sq. Ft.

| min | max |   | any ⇕ |   | min | max |

**Monday May 20**

**A** $500 1BR 1BA quiet loc., pkg garage, W/D machines, elevator. Small pets OK. (Northwest Houston)

**B** $650 2BR 1BA beautiful apt with new wood flrs., off-street pkg. No pets. (River Oaks area)

**C** $800 2BR minutes from downtown, util. incl., Brand new eat-in kitchen. Pool, alarm system.
   (Inner loop area)

**D** $450 1BR close to trans., ldry in bldg., 3rd flr walk-up. First month free! (Heights)

**E** $900 2BR 1BA beautiful apt. with yd, off-street pkg. No pets.

---

**$900 2BR 1BA beautiful apt. with yd, off-street pkg. No pets.**

Posted: Monday May 20, 10:54 am

This beautiful apartment in a quiet complex has it all, with two large bedrooms, a full bathroom with a large bathtub, and a separate dining room. Large closets in both bedrooms and a coat closet in the front entry provide plenty of storage. Carpeting is tastefully done throughout the apartment for quiet comfort. Double doors from the living room lead to your own private yard. The small parking lot next to the building is reserved for tenants. The apartment is within walking distance of River Oaks Shopping Center.

Amenities include: dishwasher, ceiling fan, microwave.

Please call 832-555-8900 for more information.

map     floor plan     photos

Ad placed by: Owner / property manager

**B** Match the words from the box with the abbreviations.

| | | | | | |
|---|---|---|---|---|---|
| a. | apartment | f. | included | k. | parking |
| b. | bathroom | g. | laundry | l. | transportation |
| c. | bedroom | h. | location | m. | utilities |
| d. | building | i. | maximum | n. | washer and dryer |
| e. | floor | j. | minimum | o. | yard |

1. _____ min.       6. _____ pkg.       11. _____ incl.

2. _____ max.       7. _____ W/D        12. _____ trans.

3. _____ BR.        8. _____ apt.       13. _____ ldry.

4. _____ BA.        9. _____ yd.        14. _____ bldg.

5. _____ loc.      10. _____ util.      15. _____ flr.

**C** Read the apartment listings again. Complete the sentences. Write the letter of the correct apartment.

1. Apartment _____ has a yard.

2. Apartment _____ is near transportation.

3. Apartment _____ has new wood floors.

4. The rent for Apartment _____ includes the cost of gas and electricity.

**D** Read the full listing for the River Oaks apartment. Check [✓] the features and amenities that it has.

a. ☐ bathtub               e. ☐ carpeting          i. ☐ dishwasher

b. ☐ eat-in kitchen        f. ☐ wood floors        j. ☐ microwave

c. ☐ separate dining room  g. ☐ yard               k. ☐ washer and dryer

d. ☐ storage space         h. ☐ parking garage     l. ☐ ceiling fan

## PRACTICAL LISTENING

**A** ◀)) Alina went to see one of the apartments. Listen to the agent describing the apartment. Which apartment is he describing: A, B, C, D, or E?

**B** ◀)) Listen again. Check [✓] the features this apartment has.

a. ☐ wood floors       d. ☐ separate dining room   g. ☐ electric stove

b. ☐ carpeting         e. ☐ dishwasher             h. ☐ bathtub

c. ☐ eat-in kitchen    f. ☐ gas stove              i. ☐ washer and dryer

## WHAT DO YOU THINK?

**GROUPS OF 3** Read the information about Alina. Look at the apartment rental listings again. Which of these apartments do you think is the best choice for Alina? Explain your answer.

> Alina's children have grown up and moved out. She and her husband are looking for a smaller apartment. They have no pets. They have a car. Usually Alina drives to work and her husband takes the bus to his job downtown. Their children visit them every weekend and stay for dinner.

## Ask about an apartment for rent

### GET READY TO WATCH

Alina is calling a property manager about an apartment for rent. What questions do you think Alina will ask about the apartment?

### WATCH

◼◀ **Watch the video. Read the statements. Circle *True* or *False*. Correct the false statements.**

| | | |
|---|---|---|
| 1. Alina is calling about a one-bedroom apartment. | True | False |
| 2. Alina asks about a washer/dryer connection. | True | False |
| 3. The apartment is available immediately. | True | False |
| 4. Alina will go and see the apartment after work. | True | False |

### CONVERSATION

**A** ◼◀ **Watch part of the video. Complete the conversation.**

**Alina:** Hi. I'm calling about the two-bedroom apartment for rent on Huldy Street.

**Manager:** Just a moment . . . 1500 Huldy? That one is still available.

The _____ is $900 a month. Would you like to see it?

**Alina:** Maybe. Can you tell me more about it?

**Manager:** Let's see. It's on the first floor. Nice building . . . quiet. There's a

_____ room, a patio, and a full bath.

**Alina:** Is there a high-speed Internet connection?

**Manager:** Yes, there is.

**Alina:** Does the building have a _____ room?

**Manager:** No. But there's a laundromat on the next block.

**B** ◀)) **Listen and repeat.**

**C** PAIRS **Practice the conversation.**

**D** PAIRS **Make similar conversations.
Ask about other apartment features and building amenities.**

### WHAT DO YOU THINK?

GROUPS OF 3 What apartment features and building amenities are the most important to you? Explain your answer.

# JOB-SEEKING SKILLS

## Complete a job application

## GET READY

Mario is completing a job application with his employment history. What kind of information do you think the application will ask for?

## READmarkdown A JOB APPLICATION

 **A** Read part of a job application. What did Mario do before working at a hospital?

List all jobs, full- or part-time, self-employment, and military service. Begin with your present or most recent position. If extra space is needed, list jobs on back of application.

| Company Name, Address, and Tel. No. | FT/PT | Dates Employed | Salary (Base Rate) | Position | Supervisor Name and Title | Reason for Leaving |
|---|---|---|---|---|---|---|
| Greenwood Heights Hospital Waco, TX 76700 254-555-9977 | FT | July 2008 to April 2013 | $19 / hr | LVN | Billie Sue Mayer, Head Nurse | moved |
| Greenwood Heights Hospital (see above) | PT | June 2003 – July 2008 | $10 / hr. | Nurse's Aide | same as above | finished LVN degree |
| Hamburger Heaven 1357 Main St. Waco, TX 76700 254-555-4828 | PT | Sept 2001 – June 2003 | $5.50 / hr. | Cook | Chuck Dillon, Branch Manager | finished high school |

**B** Read the job application again. Answer the questions.

1. When did Mario start working at Greenwood Heights Hospital? _____
2. When did Mario start working a full-time job for the first time? _____
3. How much money did Mario earn per hour as an LVN? _____
4. Why did Mario leave his last job? _____

## PUT YOUR IDEAS TO WORK

Complete part of a job application with your own employment history.

| Company Name, Address, and Tel. No. | FT/PT | Dates Employed | Salary (Base Rate) | Position | Supervisor Name and Title | Reason for Leaving |
|---|---|---|---|---|---|---|
| | | | | | | |
| | | | | | | |

## GRAMMAR

In this unit, you studied:

- Gerunds and infinitives
- Gerunds after prepositions

See page 149 for your Grammar Review.

## VOCABULARY   See page 164 for the Unit 5 Vocabulary.

**Vocabulary Learning Strategy: Make Word Webs**

**A**  Look at the words in the circles below. Make word webs with words from the Unit 5 Word List. For example.

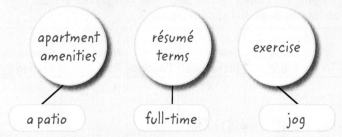

**B**  Underline five words in Exercise A. Write a sentence with each word.

## SPELLING   See page 164 for the Unit 5 Vocabulary.

**CLASS  Choose ten words for a spelling test.**

## LISTENING PLUS

**A**  Watch each video. Write the story of Alina's day.

> Alina met her coworker Ida in the hospital break room. They talked about their favorite snacks and also their exercise habits.

**B**  PAIRS  **Review the Lesson 1 conversation.** See page 62. **Role play the conversation for the class.**

## NOW I CAN

PAIRS  See page 61 for the Unit 5 Goals.  Check ☑ the things you can do.
Underline the things you want to study more. Tell your partner.

> I can _____. I need more practice with _____.

# 6 Biata Helps Out

## MY GOALS

- ☐ Assign tasks at work
- ☐ Complete a medical history form
- ☐ Take phone messages
- ☐ Call to change an appointment
- ☐ Find job resources at the library

Go to MyEnglishLab for more practice after each lesson.

**Biata Nowicki**

Biata       *Today*

My manager, Ida, is planning a big meeting. I'm sure I'll be busy today!

## Assign tasks at work

### GET READY TO WATCH

Ida is asking Biata to do some things for her. At your job, how does your manager assign you tasks for the day?

### WATCH

■◀ **Watch the video. Read the statements. Circle** *True* **or** *False*. **Correct the false statements.**

| | | | |
|---|---|---|---|
| **1.** | Ida is inviting Biata to attend a meeting. | True | False |
| **2.** | Ida asks Biata to scan some files. | True | False |
| **3.** | Biata needs to get an email address from Ida. | True | False |
| **4.** | Biata needs to send the scans on Wednesday. | True | False |
| **5.** | Biata is going to check the supply room for binders. | True | False |

### CONVERSATION

**(A)** ■◀ **Watch part of the video. Complete the conversation.**

**Ida:** I need you to take care of a few things for me. Do you have some time?

**Biata:** Of course. What can I help with?

**Ida:** First, could you scan these files and email them to Roberta Suárez over at Bay Side?

**Biata:** Sure. Where can I find Roberta's email address?

**Ida:** I'll have to look it up. Come by my _____ when you're ready to send the email.

**Biata:** OK. And when do we need to get this to her?

**Ida:** The meeting is on Wednesday, so I'd like her to have the files by Monday. That way she'll have plenty of time to review them before the _____.

**Biata:** I understand. In that case, I'll send the scans by the end of the day today.

**(B)** ◀)) **Listen and repeat.**

**(C)** PAIRS **Practice the conversation.**

**(D)** PAIRS **Make similar conversations. Assign different tasks.**

### WHAT DO YOU THINK?

GROUPS OF 3 In the video, what questions does Biata ask Ida about her work? How does Biata prioritize these tasks? Why is it important to ask questions and set priorities?

## Making requests

 **STUDY** Making requests

### Questions: Modals Can/Will/Could/Would

| Modal | *you* | Base Form | |
|---|---|---|---|
| Can | | call | these patients? |
| Will | you | | |
| Could | | copy | this file? |
| Would | | finish | the report? |

### Short Answers

| Affirmative | Negative |
|---|---|
| Yes, of course. | I'm sorry, but I can't. |
| Sure. | I'm afraid I can't. |
| No problem. | |

### Questions: *Would You Mind*

| Would you mind | Gerund | |
|---|---|---|
| Would you mind | checking | the database? |
| | helping | me? |

### Short Answers

| Affirmative | Negative |
|---|---|
| No, not at all. | I'm sorry, but I can't. |
| Of course not. | I'm afraid I can't. |

**Grammar Note**

*Could* and *Would* are more polite than *Will* and *Can*. *Would you mind* is the most polite. It is polite to use the word *please* with requests. *Please* can come before the verb or at the end of the sentence: *Can you please help me? Can you help me please?*

 **PRACTICE**

**A** Complete the conversations with the request words in parentheses. Add the subject and change the verb form when necessary. Then complete the responses.

1. **A:** (Can, send) _____ Can you send _____ this report to all the doctors?

   **B:** Yes, of _____ course _____.

2. **A:** (Would you mind, wait) _____ here for a few minutes?

   **B:** Not _____.

3. **A:** (Will, collect) _____ please _____ the lunch trays?

   **B:** I'm _____, but I can't. I have to leave before the end of lunch.

**B** Rewrite the requests on a separate piece of paper. Use the words in parentheses.

1. (Could) Please email all of these insurance companies.

   > Could you please email all of these insurance companies?

2. (Would you mind) Please stay 15 minutes later tonight.

3. (Would) Finish your report before you leave, please.

4. (Will) Please send the information to the person's home address.

**WHAT ABOUT YOU?**

**PAIRS** Write 5 tasks you want someone to do for you. Ask your partner politely to do them.

# 3 Complete a medical history form

 **GET READY**

Biata is entering information from a patient's medical history form into the database.
Guess: What type of information is on the form?

**PRACTICAL READING**

**A** Read the patient's medical history form. Was your guess correct?

## MEDICAL HISTORY

| Last Name | First Name | Date of Birth | Gender | Marital Status |
|---|---|---|---|---|
| CHOI | JENNY | 9/28/68 | FEMALE | MARRIED |

| Address | City, State | Zip Code | Telephone |
|---|---|---|---|
| 2108 BERRY ST. APT. 301 | HOUSTON, TX | 77004 | (281) 555-4982 |

In Case of Emergency, Contact:         Telephone
MIN CHOI                    (281) 555-8121

| Employer | Occupation | Social Security # |
|---|---|---|
| HAIR TRENDS | HAIR STYLIST | 000-28-7014 |

| Employer's Address | Work Telephone |
|---|---|
| 3815 KIRBY DR., HOUSTON, TX, 77098 | (281) 555-2898 |

| Insurance Company | Policy # |
|---|---|
| ASSURE HEALTH | 10956338 |

**GENERAL HEALTH**

1. Has there been any change in your health in the past year? (YES)  NO
If yes, explain: INSOMNIA, WEIGHT LOSS, BACK PAIN

2. Are you taking any medication now?               (YES)  NO
If yes, what drugs or medication? IBUPROFEN PAIN RELIEVER

3. Do you have allergic reactions to any drugs?       (YES)  NO
If yes, which drugs? PENICILLIN

4. Have you ever been hospitalized, or had a serious illness?   YES  (NO)
If yes, explain: _____

**PERSONAL MEDICAL HISTORY**

Have you ever had any of the following medical conditions?

☐ Alcoholism          ☐ Cancer          ☐ Depression

☐ Diabetes            ☐ Migraines       ☐ Tuberculosis

☐ Osteoporosis        ☑ High blood pressure

☐ Other (please list) _____

**B** Read the medical history form again. Answer the questions.

1. What is the name of the patient's insurance company? _____

2. What recent health changes does the patient report? _____

3. Has the patient ever had a serious illness? _____

4. Which drug is the patient allergic to? _____

5. What medical condition does the patient suffer from? _____

## PRACTICAL LISTENING

**A** ◀))) **Listen to a conversation between a doctor and a patient. What information does the doctor ask about? Check [✓] all correct answers.**

☐ Patient's insurance company

☐ Patient's medical history

☐ Patient's current health habits

**B** ◀))) **Listen again. Complete the medical history form with Mr. Smith's information.**

---

### GENERAL HEALTH

1. Has there been any change in your health in the past year?    YES    NO

If yes, explain: _____

2. Are you taking any medication now?    YES    NO

If yes, what drugs or medication? _____

3. Do you have allergic reactions to any drugs?    YES    NO

If yes, which drugs? _____

4. Have you ever been hospitalized, or had a serious illness?    YES    NO

If yes, explain: _____

### PERSONAL MEDICAL HISTORY

Have you ever had any of the following medical conditions?

☐ Alcoholism          ☐ Cancer          ☐ Depression

☐ Diabetes          ☐ Migraines          ☐ Tuberculosis

☐ Osteoporosis          ☐ High blood pressure

☐ Other (please list) _____

---

**C** **PAIRS** Check your answers. Compare the forms you completed in Exercise B.

## WHAT DO YOU THINK?

**GROUPS OF 3** Studies show that 30% of patients lie to their doctors about their health habits. Why do you think patients don't tell the truth about exercise, diet, and smoking habits? Why is it important to be honest with your health care providers?

# LISTENING AND SPEAKING

## Take phone messages

### GET READY TO WATCH

Biata is taking a phone message for Ida. When was the last time you took a message for someone? Who was the message for?

### WATCH

■◀ **Watch the video. Circle the correct answers.**

1. Ida is _____.
   a. in a meeting      b. out to lunch      c. gone for the day

2. The caller wants to talk to Ida about _____.
   a. a database      b. an agenda      c. a report

3. Biata is going to _____.
   a. call Ida      b. email a report      c. plan a meeting

4. Biata confirms the caller's _____.
   a. phone number      b. mailing address      c. email address

### CONVERSATION

 **A**

■◀ **Watch part of the video. Complete the conversation.**

**Biata:** Park View Hospital. Pre-op. Can I help you?

**Roberta:** Hi. This is Roberta Suárez, the administrative director from Bay Side Medical Center. I'm trying to reach Ida Harris.

**Biata:** I'm sorry. Ida is in a _____ at the moment. Can I give her a message?

**Roberta:** Sure. I'm calling about the agenda for our meeting on Wednesday. I was hoping to talk through a few things with her.

**Biata:** OK. I can have her call you as soon as she's back at her

_____. She should be back in about 20 minutes.

**Roberta:** Great. I'll wait for her call, then.

**B** ◀⟯⟯ **Listen and repeat.**

**C** PAIRS **Practice the conversation. Use your own names.**

**D** PAIRS **Make similar conversations. Imagine you are calling a teacher or classmate. Leave a different message.**

---

**Pronunciation Note**

In conversation, we often drop the /h/ sound in words like *her*, *his*, and *him*. We link the rest of the word to the word that comes before it.

◀⟯⟯ **Listen and repeat.**

Can I give her a message?

I can have her call you as soon as

she's back at her desk.

---

### WHAT DO YOU THINK?

GROUPS OF 3 These days, most people have a voicemail box or answering machine where people can leave messages. Do you think it is still valuable to leave a message with a real person?

**5**

## Indirect objects

### STUDY Indirect objects

|         | Verb | Direct Object | Preposition + Object of Preposition |
|---------|------|---------------|-------------------------------------|
| Can you | send | a report      | to Roberta? (noun object)           |
|         |      |               | to her? (object pronoun)            |

|       | Verb       | Indirect Object | Direct Object |
|-------|------------|-----------------|---------------|
| Biata | is sending | Roberta         | a report.     |
|       |            | her             |               |

> **Grammar Note**
>
> Indirect objects can only follow certain verbs. Here are some common ones:
> *show, give, send, buy, bring, tell, make, cook, get, cost, ask, hand, pay, lend, teach.*

See page 160 for a review of object pronouns.

### PRACTICE

**A** Rewrite the sentences on a separate piece of paper.
Change the indirect object from a noun to a pronoun.

1. Ida sent Biata a reminder message.

   *Ida sent her a reminder message.*

2. Biata gave Ida the message from Roberta.
3. The nurses got Frank a small gift for his birthday.
4. Frank wrote the nurses a thank-you note.
5. The doctor wrote my mother a new prescription.

**B** Rewrite the sentences on a separate piece of paper.
Change the object of the preposition into an indirect object.

1. Paul is going to bring a basket of fruit to Lisa's family when he visits them.

   *Paul is going to bring Lisa's family a basket of fruit when he visits them.*

2. Tina wants to give a watch to her father on his birthday this year.
3. I'll buy a coffee for you during our break.
4. Jim brought flowers to his grandmother in the hospital.
5. Are you going to send a gift to your friend for his birthday?

### WHAT ABOUT YOU?

**PAIRS** Talk about things you want to *give, send, bring,* or *buy* people.
Use object pronouns as indirect objects.

*I want to buy something for my mother's birthday. I'm going to buy her a scarf.*

# Make inferences

## GET READY

Biata is taking an online quiz about how to talk to a doctor. Do you sometimes have trouble talking to your doctor at an appointment?

## READM

◀))) **Listen and read the doctor-patient communication quiz.**
**Why is it important to communicate with your health care providers?**

### How Well Do You Communicate with Your Doctor?

Many of us have trouble talking to our health care providers. However, research shows that patients who share information with their doctors get better results and stay healthier. So how well do you communicate with your health care providers? Take this quiz and find out!

#### Doctor-Patient Communication Quiz

**Answer the questions. Write "A" (always), "S" (sometimes), or "N" (never) on the line.**

When you visit a doctor, how often do you . . .

1. make a list of what you want to talk about before your visit? _____
2. tell your doctor your biggest concerns at the start of the visit? _____
3. bring a friend or family member for support? _____
4. speak frankly about your symptoms, even if they're embarrassing? _____
5. give honest answers about your health habits and lifestyle? _____
6. ask questions if you don't understand what the doctor said? _____
7. ask your doctor to write down his or her instructions? _____
8. ask why your doctor is giving you a prescription? _____
9. ask if a drug has any side effects? _____
10. ask if there are other treatment options available? _____
11. ask if a medical test is necessary, and what the test will tell you? _____
12. ask how long it will be until you feel better? _____
13. ask for an interpreter if you have trouble understanding English? _____
14. ask to communicate later by phone if you have more questions? _____
15. ask where you can get more information about your illness? _____

#### Scoring

Give yourself: 2 points for each "always" answer
1 point for each "sometimes" answer
0 points for each "never" answer

**0–9  points:** You really need to work on your communication skills.

**10–19 points:** Not bad, but you may want to speak up a little more.

**20–30 points:** Nice job! You're an active member of your own health care team.

## AFTER YOU READ

**A** **Read the doctor-patient communication quiz again. Take the quiz and score your results.**

**B** **Read the Reading Skill. Complete the statements based on your inferences from the text.**

1. This article is probably from an online _____.
   **a.** children's website    **b.** medical website    **c.** social or friends' website

2. The article suggests that communication between doctors and patients _____.
   **a.** is excellent    **b.** never happens    **c.** needs improving

3. The article suggests that the questions in the quiz can help you learn to communicate with your doctor _____.
   **a.** in a better way    **b.** in a worse way    **c.** in the same way

## VOCABULARY STUDY  Collocations

**Build Your Vocabulary**

A **collocation** is a grouping of two or more words that are frequently used together. This combination of the words sounds natural to native speakers. For example, the words *do* and *the dishes* are often used together in natural speech.

| Collocations | | | |
|---|---|---|---|
| **Verb + Noun** | **Adverb + Verb** | **Adjective + Noun** | **Adverb + Adjective** |
| make a mistake | totally agree | fast food | wide awake |

**Read the Build Your Vocabulary note.**
**Then match the words that are used together in the article.**

_____ **1.** treatment        **a.** provider

_____ **2.** take             **b.** effects

_____ **3.** active           **c.** a quiz

_____ **4.** communication    **d.** options

_____ **5.** side             **e.** skills

_____ **6.** health care      **f.** member

## WHAT DO YOU THINK?

**PAIRS** Do you think the quiz gives good advice for communicating with health care providers? Do you agree with your quiz results? Explain your answers.

**ON THE WEB**

For more information, go online and search "tips for talking to your doctor." Find a new suggestion and report back to the class.

# Write a narrative paragraph

## GET READY

Biata is writing an email to an old friend. Do you communicate with your friends by email? How regularly do you write to them? What do you write about?

## STUDY THE MODEL

**A** **Read the email. What does Biata tell her friend about?**

Hi, Jenna.

It was great to hear from you. It's been a long time since I last saw you! It sounds like everything is going really well.

You asked how I'm doing at work. Well, today was unbelievable. I'm home now, and I'm exhausted. This morning, the first thing that happened was that my coworker Judy called in sick. So I had to work alone at the desk. Then my boss, Ida, called me in. She asked me to do some things for her. We are planning for a big meeting, and she wants everything in order. When I got back to my desk, there were so many messages on my phone! While I was calling people back, some new patients came in, and I had to help them complete their forms. At lunchtime I was able to get away and relax a bit. After that, the afternoon continued to be very busy. I had to file more papers, make more phone calls, and enter more patient information into the database. By 4 o'clock I was pretty tired, and I still had to organize the stockroom. Finally, I had three patients to call to remind them about their appointments.

Not every day is like this, though. Today was just one of those days!

Warm regards,
Biata

> **Writing Tip**
>
> When writing a narrative paragraph, use **phrases of time and place** such as *In the morning* or *Back at home*. This will help make it clear when and where the events happen. It will make it easier for readers to follow your story.

**B** **Read the Writing Tip. Then read Biata's email in Exercise A again. Underline 5 phrases of time or place.**

**C** **PAIRS** Compare your answers to Exercise B.

**D** **Look at the timeline Biata used to plan her email, and complete it.**

**TODAY**

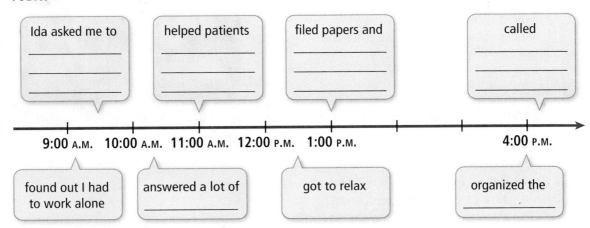

Ida asked me to
_____
_____

helped patients
_____
_____

filed papers and
_____
_____

called
_____
_____
_____

9:00 A.M.  10:00 A.M.  11:00 A.M.  12:00 P.M.  1:00 P.M.          4:00 P.M.

found out I had
to work alone

answered a lot of
_____

got to relax

organized the
_____

## BEFORE YOU WRITE

You're going to write an email telling a friend what you did yesterday.
Complete a timeline to plan your email. Add times or dates to the timeline.
Write your actions in the balloons.

**YESTERDAY**

## WRITE

Review the Model and the Writing Tip. Use the ideas from your timeline to write your
email to a friend. Include phrases of time and place to make it clear when and where
the events happened.

# 8 Call to change an appointment

## GET READY TO WATCH

A patient is calling Biata to change his appointment. What are some common reasons for changing an appointment?

## WATCH

◀ **Watch the video. Circle the correct answers.**

**1.** When does the patient want to come in?

    **a.** tomorrow     **b.** later this week     **c.** early next week

**2.** What does the patient ask Biata?

    **a.** How long until the next opening?

    **b.** How long does the appointment last?

    **c.** How long does it take to get there?

**3.** Why does the patient need to come early for the appointment?

    **a.** to fill out some forms     **b.** to meet the doctor     **c.** to get an insurance card

## CONVERSATION

**A** ◀ **Watch part of the video.
Complete the conversation.**

**Biata:** Hello, Park View Hospital, Pre-op. Can I help you?

**Patient:** Yes. This is Brian Lee. I have an appointment

    _____, but I can't make it.

**Biata:** Brian Lee. . . . Yes, I see it. A consultation with Dr. Bronson. Do you want to reschedule?

**Patient:** Yes, I do. Can I come in early next

    _____?

**Biata:** Let's see. . . . Yes. How about Tuesday at 10 A.M.?

**Patient:** Oh. I can't make it on Tuesday _____.
But I'm free in the afternoon. . . .

**Biata:** OK. . . . Tuesday afternoon? We have an opening at 3 o'clock.

**Patient:** Yes, that's fine.

### Pronunciation Note

The most common vowel sound in English is the short, unclear vowel /ə/. We use /ə/ in many unstressed syllables and short unstressed words.

◀)) **Listen and repeat.**

an appointment

I have an appointment tomorrow.

o'clock

We have an opening at 3 o'clock.

**B** ◀)) **Listen and repeat.**

**C** **PAIRS** **Practice the conversation. Use your own names.**

**D** **PAIRS** **Make similar conversations. Use other days and times.**

## WHAT DO YOU THINK?

**GROUPS OF 3** Some offices charge patients a fee for rescheduling less than 24 hours before an appointment. Do you think this is fair?

# JOB-SEEKING SKILLS

## Find job resources at the library

**Mario López** *Today*
I'm on the Job Resource web page of my local library. I need some help with my job search!

### GET READY

Mario is looking for resources to help him in his job search.
What resources do you think the library might have?

### FIND JOB RESOURCES AT THE LIBRARY

**A** **Mario is reading a page on his library website. He has already completed some applications. Which of these library resources would be most useful to Mario as a next step?**

---

**Houston Public Library**     Home | Catalog | Locations | Events | Kids | About

Welcome to the Job Resource Center! Here you'll find everything you need to put you on the path to finding a job. Click on the links below for more information.

**Learn the basics** FREE classes, references, and resources to help you learn some basic skills and find out about available jobs.

**Explore career options** Discover careers. Learn about training programs. Assess your job skills.

**Build your résumé** Take our online tutorial or get one-on-one help to create your résumé. Look at examples of cover letters.

**Find a job** Learn about where to look for jobs, or come to a free networking session.

**Prepare for an interview** Learn what you need to know for a successful interview. Or look at links to some online interviewing tips.

**Learn about unemployment benefits** Learn what benefits you are eligible for. Get help filing your claim online.

---

**B** ◀)) **Mario visits the public library. Listen to his conversation with a librarian about the resources available. Check [✓] which resources the librarian mentions.**

☐ job listings
☐ free email address
☐ free phone number
☐ computer classes
☐ English classes
☐ math classes

☐ information about salaries
☐ information about training requirements
☐ tutors to help with training for a job
☐ tutors to help prepare a résumé
☐ free computer time
☐ tips on successful interviews

### PUT YOUR IDEAS TO WORK

**PAIRS** Imagine you are looking for a job. Which of the resources in Exercise B would be the most valuable for you? Explain your answer.

**ON THE WEB**

For more information, go online to your local library website. Find 3 job search resources and report back to the class.

## GRAMMAR

In this unit, you studied:

- Modals *Can/Will/Could/Would* for requests
- Indirect objects

See page 150 for your Grammar Review.

## VOCABULARY  See page 164 for the Unit 6 Vocabulary.

**Vocabulary Learning Strategy: Group Words by Number of Syllables**

**A**  Choose words from the Unit 6 Word List with 1 to 5 syllables. Write them in the chart.

| One syllable | Two syllables | Three syllables | Four syllables | Five syllables |
|---|---|---|---|---|
| file | binder | agenda | insomnia | tuberculosis |
| | | | | |
| | | | | |
| | | | | |
| | | | | |

**B**  Underline 5 words in Exercise A. Write a sentence with each word.

## SPELLING  See page 164 for the Unit 6 Vocabulary.

**CLASS**  Choose 10 words for a spelling test.

## LISTENING PLUS

**A**  Watch each video. Write the story of Biata's day.

*Biata met her supervisor Ida. Ida asked Biata to help her prepare for a meeting.*

**B**  **PAIRS**  Review the Lesson 8 conversation. See page 86. Role play the conversation for the class.

## NOW I CAN

**PAIRS**  See page 75 for the Unit 6 Goals.  Check ☑ the things you can do.
Underline the things you want to study more. Tell your partner.

> I can _____. I need more practice with _____.

# 7 Frank Makes Time

## MY GOALS

☐ Give multi-step instructions

☐ Give a progress report at work

☐ Read a work schedule

☐ Ask to change shifts with someone

☐ Answer common interview questions

Go to MyEnglishLab for more practice after each lesson.

**Frank Sánchez**
Frank                    *Today*
I need to change my schedule. I hope someone can change shifts with me.

# 1

## Give multi-step instructions

## GET READY TO WATCH

Frank is giving instructions to Sagar, a new worker. When was the last time you had to tell someone how to do something?

## WATCH

◼◀ **Watch the video. Number the instructions in the order Frank gives them.**

1. _____ Knock on a patient's door.
2. _____ Double-check the diet card.
3. _____ Put the diet card on the tray.
4. _____ Deliver the tray to the patient.
5. _____ Load the tray on the cart.
6. _____ Knock again if the patient doesn't answer.

## CONVERSATION

**A** ◼◀ **Watch part of the video. Complete the conversation.**

**Frank:** Let's begin with tray preparation. As you are getting each _____ ready, be sure to double-check the diet card.

**Sagar:** Check the diet card.

**Frank:** Right. It gives the patient's diet type and food preferences, so it's really important to get that right.

**Sagar:** OK. I'll be sure to do that.

**Frank:** Then set the diet _____ at the side of the tray. After you prepare the tray,

load it onto the _____.
You can put two trays on each level of the cart.

**Sagar:** Sorry—did you say "two to a level"?

**Frank:** Yes, that's right.

### Pronunciation Note

Notice the intonation in these sentences with two clauses. The voice jumps up on the most important word in each clause. It goes down low at the end of the sentence.

◀)) **Listen and repeat.**

As you are getting each **tray** ready,
  be sure to check the **diet** card.

After you prepare the **tray**,
  load it onto the **cart**.

**B** ◀)) Listen and repeat.

**C** PAIRS Practice the conversation.

**D** PAIRS Think of a task that you need to do at home or work. What are the steps you need to take to do that task?

**E** SAME PAIRS Make similar conversations. Give instructions. Use your ideas from Exercise D.

## WHAT DO YOU THINK?

◼◀ Watch the video again. How does Sagar make sure she understands Frank's instructions?

**2** Adverb clauses of time

| Time Clause | Main Clause |
|---|---|
| **As** you prepare each tray, | check the meal card. |
| **After** you prepare the tray, | put it on the cart. |
| **Before** you go in to each room, | knock on the door. |
| **When** you serve the food, | put the tray on the bedside table. |

> **Grammar Note**
>
> You can also put the time clause after the main clause. Do not use a comma.
> *You should knock on the door before you go in.*

**PRACTICE**

**A** **On a separate piece of paper, combine the sentences into one sentence. Use the words in parentheses.**

1. You clean each tray. Check what the patient has eaten. (before)

> *Before you clean each tray, check what the patient has eaten.*

2. Check the diet card. You empty each tray. (as)
3. The bucket for dirty dishes is full. Bring it to the dishwasher. (when)
4. You put your cart back in the supply closet. Wash it down. (before)
5. You have cleaned and put away the cart. Return the diet cards to this box. (after)

**B** **Complete the instructions with the adverbs of time and the phrases from the box.**

> they are done          the eggs are cooking          ~~you don't have much time~~
> you begin               you do this                   two to five minutes

Scrambled eggs make a quick meal _when you don't have much time_.
                                          1. when

_____, you will need two eggs, some salt and pepper,
        2. before

and a tablespoon of butter. You will also need a frying pan and a spoon to stir the eggs.

First, break the eggs into a bowl. _____,
                                          3. after

beat them thoroughly with a fork. Then melt the butter in the pan on low heat. Continue

to stir _____. The eggs will be set and creamy
              4. as

_____. _____,
        5. after                          6. when

put them on a warm plate and serve immediately.

**WHAT ABOUT YOU?**

**PAIRS** Think of a task that you know how to do. Give your partner instructions for how to do it. Use adverb clauses of time.

**LESSON** **READING**

**3**

# Determine the author's purpose

## GET READY

Frank is thinking about doing some volunteer work. He reads an online interview about volunteering. Have you ever volunteered your time to help others?

## READD

◀))) **Listen and read the article. Who is Sedara Rosmund?**

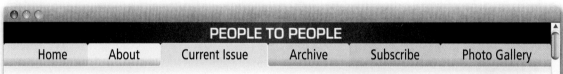

PEOPLE TO PEOPLE

| Home | About | Current Issue | Archive | Subscribe | Photo Gallery |

### Ready to Volunteer

Each year, 60 million adults volunteer their time in the U.S. These volunteers give over 8.1 billion hours to important causes. Who are these volunteers? Why do they do it? And how do they find the time? We talked with Sedara Rosmund, a volunteer with the children's literacy organization *Ready to Read*, about her experiences.

**Sedara, tell us about the *Ready to Read* program.**

Sure! We go to local elementary schools twice a week. Each volunteer works with one child. The children choose a book at the school library, and we read together for 30 minutes. The kids can choose to read aloud or just listen. We encourage them to ask questions and talk about the story. It's so interesting to hear what they have to say!

**How did you get started?**

I didn't know anything about volunteering. I wasn't even sure I had any skills that an organization would value. Then a friend mentioned that he volunteers as a youth soccer coach. He told me how much fun he has with the kids and how he meets lots of new people. I wanted to do that, too, but I don't play sports. Then I heard about *Ready to Read*. I spoke to other volunteers, and they convinced me that I actually had a lot to offer the program.

**What do you like about volunteer work?**

Everything! The best thing is that I feel I'm really helping these kids. Giving the gift of reading to a child is priceless. And it's a great experience for me, too. It gives me self-confidence. When I was interviewing for a job, the school principal wrote a letter of reference for me. The kind things she said actually made me cry.

**You have such a busy life. How do you find the time to volunteer?**

You're right. I'm so busy! It's hard to juggle my family, my job, and my classes. But when I don't volunteer, I really miss it. My life doesn't feel as full or meaningful. I think everyone should volunteer. It doesn't take much—just a few hours can really make a difference in someone's life!

## AFTER YOU READ

**A** Read the Reading Skill. Why do you think the author chose to interview Sedara Rosmund?

**B** Look at the chart about where people volunteer. Answer the questions.

## Where People Volunteer

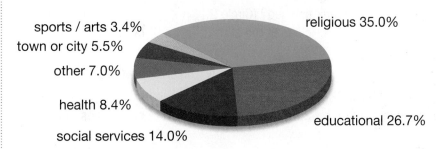

sports / arts 3.4%
town or city 5.5%
other 7.0%
health 8.4%
social services 14.0%
religious 35.0%
educational 26.7%

1. What percentage of people volunteer for social services? _____

2. What do 26.7% of people volunteer for? _____

3. Do more people volunteer for educational organizations or health organizations? _____

## VOCABULARY STUDY Word Roots

**Build Your Vocabulary**

A **word root** is the most basic form of a word. It expresses the important description, thought, or meaning and can't be broken into smaller parts. For example, the root of the word *volunteer* is *vol-*, which means *will*.

| Root | Meaning | Example | Example from the Article |
|------|---------|---------|--------------------------|
| **1.** liter- | letter(s) | literature | |
| **2.** cor-, cour- | heart | courage | |
| **3.** fid- | faith, trust | confide | |
| **4.** -view (vis-, vid-) | see | review | |

**Read the Build your Vocabulary note. Complete the chart with examples from the article.**

### WHAT DO YOU THINK?

**GROUPS OF 3** Volunteers give a lot of useful services to their communities. Do you think that volunteers also benefit from their volunteer work? Explain your answer.

**ON THE WEB**

For more information, go online and search for volunteer opportunities in your community. Find a volunteer opportunity that interests you and report back to the class.

## 4  Give a progress report at work

### GET READY TO WATCH

Frank is giving Jae a progress report on his daily tasks. Guess: What has Frank just finished doing?

### WATCH

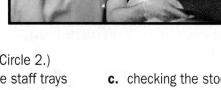

**A**  ◼◀ **Watch the video. Was your guess correct?**

**B**  ◼◀ **Watch the video again.**
**Circle the correct answers.**

1. Which of the following tasks has Frank finished? (Circle 2.)
   a. clearing the patients' trays    b. clearing the staff trays    c. checking the stock

2. What is Frank going to send Jae?
   a. a list of supplies    b. a report about new workers    c. his schedule

3. What does Frank say about Sagar?
   a. She asks too many questions.    b. She is enthusiastic.    c. He likes working with her.

### CONVERSATION

**A**  ◼◀ **Watch part of the video.**
**Complete the conversation.**

**Jae:**    Do you have a minute?

**Frank:**  Sure.

**Jae:**    Where are we with the
            _____ shift?

**Frank:**  Well, I've just cleared the trays from the patients' rooms.

**Jae:**    OK. And what about the staff dishes? Are those cleaned up, too?

**Frank:**  No, I haven't cleared those yet. I was about to do that.

**Jae:**    OK. Good. When you finish with that, could you check the cafeteria stock?

**Frank:**  Actually, I've already done that. I checked the stock this morning,
            after the _____ shift.

> **Pronunciation Note**
>
> Notice the different sounds in *she* /ʃ/ and *check* /tʃ/. You can make the sound /ʃ/ (*she*) long: /ʃʃʃ/. The sound /tʃ/ (*check*) begins with /t/ and is always short.
>
> ◀))) **Listen and repeat.**
>
> | /ʃ/ | sure | shift | patients | finish |
> | --- | --- | --- | --- | --- |
> | /tʃ/ | check | lunch | watch | questions |

**B**  ◀))) **Listen and repeat.**

**C**  PAIRS  **Practice the conversation.**

**D**  PAIRS  **Think of a job. List 3 tasks that workers with that job need to do.**

**E**  SAME PAIRS  **Make similar conversations. Use the tasks you listed in Exercise D.**

### WHAT DO YOU THINK?

**GROUPS OF 3**  In the video, Frank checks the stock when he has extra time, even though Jae doesn't ask him to do that. What is the value of staying busy when you are at work?

Present perfect with *already* and *yet*

 **STUDY** Present perfect with *already* and *yet*

**Already: Affirmative Statements**

| Subject | *have* | *already* | Past Participle | |
|---|---|---|---|---|
| I | have | already | served | lunch. |
| Frank | has | | cleared | the trays. |

**Grammar Note**

In affirmative statements, *already* can also come at the end of the sentence. *Already* is sometimes used in questions. It indicates surprise.

**Yet: Negative Statements**

| Subject | *have not* | Past Participle | | *yet* |
|---|---|---|---|---|
| I | haven't | cleaned | the kitchen | yet. |
| Maria | hasn't | started | her shift | |

**Yet: Questions**

| Have | you | washed | the dishes | yet? |
|---|---|---|---|---|

**Short Answers**

| Yes, I **have**. | No, I **haven't**. |
|---|---|

**PRACTICE**

**A** Complete the conversations. Use the present perfect form of the verbs and *already* or *yet*. Complete the short answers.

1. **A:** I see you _____have already prepared_____ (prepare) Room 324.

   **B:** Yes, _____. When is the patient arriving?

   **A.** He _____ (not complete) the registration form _____.
   I expect it will be another half hour.

2. **A:** _____ Jae _____ (arrive) _____?

   **B:** Yes, _____. He is in the kitchen.

   **A:** Oh, good. He _____ (not give) me my shift time for the weekend

   _____.

   **B:** I think he _____ (finish) the chart. I'm sure he'll talk to you soon.

**B** Look at Frank's to-do list. Write sentences about what Frank has already finished and what he hasn't done yet. Use a separate piece of paper.

| ✓ Check the stock |
|---|
| Talk to Alina about the new patients |
| ✓ Call about the bad fruit delivery |
| Ask John about lunch |
| Pick up the car |

Frank has already checked the stock.

**WHAT ABOUT YOU?**

**PAIRS** Talk about the things you have already done today.
Talk about the things you plan to do later but haven't done yet.

# Write a descriptive email

## GET READY

Frank and his manager, Jae, visit a hospital in Corpus Christi to observe their food service department. When was the last time you visted a new place? What were the most interesting things about it?

## STUDY THE MODEL

**A** Frank sends an email to his wife, Carla, while he is away. Read Frank's email. What does Frank like about Corpus Christi?

---

**Subject:** Learning a lot on my trip!

Hi Carla,

I hope you are doing well and everything is OK at home. I really like Corpus Christi so far. It's a beautiful city. The ocean is always nearby. This morning I woke up to the sound of the waves on the beach. It was so peaceful and relaxing. And when I looked out the window, I saw the sun rising across the bay. The water was sparkling. It looked so clean and fresh. I felt like I was on vacation, not here for work!

But of course, I've been really busy here. Jae and I went to Oceanside Hospital today to observe their food service department. The hospital's new cafeteria opened today. It's really nice. They put a lot of thought into it. The first thing I noticed when I arrived in the cafeteria was the smell of bread baking. The cafeteria has a bakery, and they make cinnamon rolls every morning. The rolls taste as good as they smell. They're so sweet and buttery. There are other nice things about the cafeteria, too. They have art on the walls showing beach scenes, and they play quiet, calming music. When Jae and I get back to Park View, we're going to try out some of these ideas.

After a long day at the hospital, we returned to the hotel for a break before dinner. I went down to the beach alone to relax. I walked along the beach for an hour or so. The sand was still warm from the sun. It felt great to sift it through my hands. I also found a lot of beautiful shells which are as smooth as glass and have rich colors. I'm bringing some home for you.

I miss you and wish you were here. Next time, let's plan a vacation here if we can!

Your loving husband,

Frank

---

**B** Read the Writing Tip.
Then read Frank's email again.
Underline the descriptive adjectives.

> ### Writing Tip
>
> Use **descriptive adjectives** to help your reader get a more complete idea of what you are writing about. Use adjectives that give information about what things *look* like, *sound* like, *smell* like, *feel* like, or *taste* like.

**C**  **Look at the ideas web Frank used to plan his email, and complete it.**

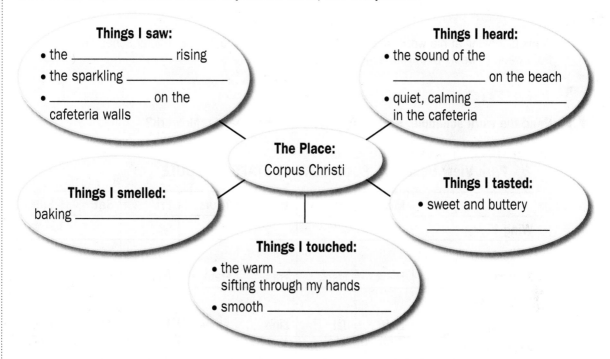

**Things I saw:**
- the _____ rising
- the sparkling _____
- _____ on the cafeteria walls

**Things I heard:**
- the sound of the _____ on the beach
- quiet, calming _____ in the cafeteria

**The Place:**
Corpus Christi

**Things I smelled:**
baking _____

**Things I tasted:**
- sweet and buttery _____

**Things I touched:**
- the warm _____ sifting through my hands
- smooth _____

## BEFORE YOU WRITE

You're going to write an email to a friend about a new place you have visited. Think of the five senses. Create an ideas web to plan your email.

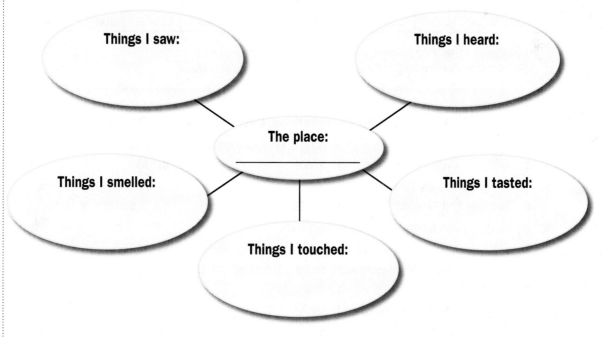

**Things I saw:**

**Things I heard:**

**The place:**
_____

**Things I smelled:**

**Things I tasted:**

**Things I touched:**

## WRITE

Review the Model and the Writing Tip. Use the ideas from your ideas web to write an email to a friend describing the place you chose.

## Read a work schedule

**GET READY**

Frank is looking at his work schedule for next week. Do you have a regular schedule from week to week, or is your schedule flexible?

**PRACTICAL READING**

 Read the work schedule. How many days per week does Frank work?

### Park View Hospital  FOOD SERVICE STAFF SCHEDULE

|  | Mon | Tues | Wed | Thurs | Fri | Sat | Sun |
|---|---|---|---|---|---|---|---|
| **Wing 1** | | | | | | | |
| 7:00 A.M.–3:00 P.M. | Frank | Frank | Frank | Frank | Frank | Mai | Mai |
| 11:00 A.M.–7:00 P.M. | Linh | Tal | Linh | Amber | Tal | Amber | Amber |
| **Wing 2** | | | | | | | |
| 7:00 A.M.–3:00 P.M. | Maria | Maria | Sagar | Sagar | Maria | Maria | Maria |
| 11:00 A.M.–7:00 P.M. | Charlie | Tomás | Charlie | Tomás | Charlie | Tomás | Tomás |

*Lunch break 12:30–1:00 for morning shift; 1:00–1:30 for afternoon shift
15-minute break mid-morning and mid-afternoon (check with Frank or Maria)

**B** Read the schedule again. Answer the questions. Circle the correct answers.

**1.** Who works on the afternoon shift in Wing 1 on Mondays and Wednesdays?
    **a.** Linh        **b.** Amber        **c.** Mai

**2.** On which days does Tal work?
    **a.** Monday and Wednesday    **b.** Tuesday and Thursday    **c.** Tuesday and Friday

**3.** Which employee works only on the weekends?
    **a.** Mai        **b.** Amber        **c.** Tomás

**4.** How many different employees work in Wing 2 throughout the week?
    **a.** three        **b.** four        **c.** five

**5.** When does Charlie take his lunch break?
    **a.** 12:30        **b.** 1:00        **c.** 1:30

## PRACTICAL SPEAKING

**A** ◀))) **A worker sees a mistake on his schedule and talks to his manager about it. Listen and read the conversation. What is the mistake?**

**Dave:** Hi, Jen. I was just looking at the schedule for next week, and I think there's a mistake. I asked for Friday off next week. Remember?

**Jen:** Oh! That's right. I'm sorry, I did forget. I just copied last week's schedule.

**Dave:** Is it still OK to take that day off?

**Jen:** Yes. I'll have to figure out who can cover for you, though.

**Dave:** I can ask around, if you'd like.

**Jen:** That would be great. But if you don't find someone, don't worry. I have other people I can call in.

**Dave:** Thanks.

**B** ◀))) **Listen and repeat.**

**C** PAIRS **Dave noticed that his manager forgot to give him a day off. What are some other mistakes you might find on a work schedule?**

**D** SAME PAIRS **Role play a similar conversation between an employee and a manager. Point out a different mistake.**

## PRACTICAL LISTENING

◀))) **A Human Resources manager is explaining the schedule rules at a meeting for new employees. Listen and answer the questions.**

**1.** When are the weekly schedules posted?

_____

**2.** How early does the manager suggest people show up for their shift? _____

**3.** What should workers do before taking a break?

_____

_____

**4.** If workers need to change shifts or days, what should they do? _____

_____

## WHAT DO YOU THINK?

GROUPS OF 3 Read the paragraph about Maria's schedule. What are the benefits of Maria and her husband working different shifts? What problems do you think this can cause?

Maria works the morning shift at Park View Hospital. She has two children—a four-year-old and a six-year-old. Her husband, Eduardo, works from 4 P.M. to 12:00 A.M. at a warehouse. With this arrangement, one of them can always be home with the children.

### GET READY TO WATCH

Frank is asking Amber to change work days with him next week. What are some reasons you might want to change your schedule or ask for a day off?

### WATCH

◼◀ **Watch the video. Circle the correct answers.**

**1.** Which day does Frank want to take off?
   **a.** Thursday       **b.** Friday       **c.** Saturday

**2.** What event is happening on that day?
   **a.** his anniversary    **b.** his wife's birthday    **c.** his nephew's graduation

**3.** Which day will Amber take off?
   **a.** Friday       **b.** Saturday       **c.** Sunday

### CONVERSATION

**A**   ◼◀ **Watch part of the video. Complete the conversation.**

**Frank:**   Amber, hi. Can I ask you a favor?

**Amber:**   Of course. What is it?

**Frank:**   You don't work on Fridays, right?

**Amber:**   Right. I'm normally in _____ days a week—Thursdays, Saturdays, and Sundays.

**Frank:**   Well, my nephew's graduation is on Friday, and I want to take that day off so I can be there. Do you think we could switch days?

**Amber:**   You mean, you want me to work your _____ on Friday?

**Frank:**   Right. And then I'll work a shift for you.

**Amber:**   Sure. That sounds fine.

**Frank:**   Thanks. I appreciate it.

**B**   ◀)) **Listen and repeat.**

**C**   PAIRS **Practice the conversation. Use your own names.**

**D**   PAIRS **Make similar conversations. Ask for different days off. Use different reasons.**

### WHAT DO YOU THINK?

**GROUPS OF 3** Imagine you have a coworker who always asks to change shifts with you. He usually has a good reason, but you are getting tired of switching shifts. What do you do?

# JOB-SEEKING SKILLS

## Answer common interview questions

**Mario López** *Today*
Just got a call from Park View Hospital. They want me to come in for an interview!

## GET READY

Mario interviews for an LVN position at Park View Hospital. What are some common questions that interviewers ask?

## ANSWER COMMON INTERVIEW QUESTIONS

**A** ◀))) **Listen to the first part of Mario's interview. Check [✓] the questions you hear.**

☐ How many years of experience do you have?

☐ Can you tell me about your experience at your last job?

☐ What did you like about that job?

☐ Why are you interested in working here?

☐ Where do you see yourself in 5 years?

☐ What kinds of challenges did you have at your previous jobs?

☐ Have you ever had to resolve a difficult situation? What did you do?

☐ If you worked here, what qualities would you bring to us?

☐ What are some things about yourself that you would like to improve?

☐ Have you ever had to work with a difficult coworker? What did you do?

**B** ◀))) **Listen again. Complete the sentences.**

**1.** At his previous job, Mario was asked to _____ new staff members.

**2.** Mario is interested in working at Park View Hospital because he likes the LVN-to-RN

_____ and their _____ reimbursement program.

**3.** The interviewer asks Mario if he is concerned about working at a _____ hospital than Greenwood Heights Hospital.

**4.** Mario feels that _____ is a big challenge for LVNs.

**5.** Mario describes himself as _____ and says he likes to take on challenges.

**6.** Mario says that he used to ask for a lot of _____.

**C** **GROUPS OF 4 Do you think Mario gave good answers to the interviewer's questions? Why or why not?**

## PUT YOUR IDEAS TO WORK

**A** **Think of a job you would like to apply for, and think about your own work history. Write your answers to the questions in Exercise A.**

**B** **GROUPS OF 4 Role play job interviews. Then change roles.**
**Students A and B:** Use the questions from Exercise A and your own answers.
**Students C and D:** Observe and evaluate the interview.

## GRAMMAR

In this unit, you studied:
- Adverb clauses of time
- Present perfect with *already* and *yet*

See page 151 for your Grammar Review.

## VOCABULARY  See page 165 for the Unit 7 Vocabulary.

**Vocabulary Learning Strategy: Group Words by Part of Speech**

**A**  Choose 5 nouns and 5 verbs from the Unit 7 Word List. Write them in the chart.

| Nouns | Verbs | Adjectives |
|-------|-------|------------|
| wing | load | capable |
|  |  |  |
|  |  |  |
|  |  |  |
|  |  |  |

**B**  Underline 5 words in Exercise A. Write a sentence with each word.

## SPELLING  See page 165 for the Unit 7 Vocabulary.

**CLASS**  Choose 10 words for a spelling test.

## LISTENING PLUS

**A**  Watch each video. Write the story of Frank's day.

Frank met a new food service worker named Sagar. Frank showed Sagar how to prepare meal trays.

**B**  **PAIRS**  Review the Lesson 8 conversation. See page 100. Role play the conversation for the class.

## NOW I CAN

**PAIRS**  See page 89 for the Unit 7 Goals. Check ☑ the things you can do. Underline the things you want to study more. Tell your partner.

> I can ____. I need more practice with ____.

# 8 Susan at Work and Play

## MY GOALS

☐ Get a performance evaluation at work

☐ Ask about someone's belongings

☐ Complete a credit card application

☐ Talk about personal interests

☐ Ask questions at a job interview

Go to MyEnglishLab for more practice after each lesson.

 **Susan Kim**

**Susan** *Today*

Today is my first performance evaluation. I'm a little nervous!

oooooo ## GET READY TO WATCH

Henry is giving Susan a performance evaluation.
Have you ever had an evaluation at work?

## WATCH

◼◀ **Watch the video. Circle the correct answers.**

1. Susan's general performance is _____.
   **a.** very good   **b.** good   **c.** not good enough

2. Henry says that Susan needs to _____ patients.
   **a.** take better care of   **b.** spend less time with   **c.** develop empathy for

3. Susan _____ with the other nurses.
   **a.** spends too much time   **b.** gets along well   **c.** doesn't like working

## CONVERSATION

**A** ◼◀ **Watch part of the video. Complete the conversation.**

**Henry:** I think you've been doing a terrific job, overall. You take great _____ of the patients here.

**Susan:** Thank you. I like taking care of people. It's why I became a nurse.

**Henry:** It shows. It's clearly one of your best qualities. But there is one thing I'd like you to work on.

**Susan:** OK.

**Henry:** I've noticed that you've been spending too much _____ with certain patients. I know some of them can be pretty demanding!

**Susan:** Oh. Yes, I guess I have been giving some patients extra attention.

**Henry:** Of course, empathy is good. But you do need to maintain a professional distance.

**Susan:** Yes, I can see that. Thanks for pointing it out. I'll _____ on that.

> **Pronunciation Note**
>
> We usually use the contraction *'d* for *would* after a pronoun. Notice the /d/ sound that makes *I'd like* sound different from *I like*.
>
> ◀))) **Listen and repeat.**
> There's one thing I'd like you to work on.
> I like taking care of people.

**B** ◀))) **Listen and repeat.**

**C** **PAIRS** **Practice the conversation.**

**D** **PAIRS** **Talk about things you do well and things you could improve at your job.**

**E** **SAME PAIRS** **Make similar conversations. Role play your own performance review. Use your ideas from Exercise D.**

## WHAT DO YOU THINK?

**GROUPS OF 3** Why do employers give performance evaluations? Do you think these reviews are also valuable for employees? Explain your opinion.

# GRAMMAR

## 2 Present perfect continuous

### STUDY Present perfect continuous

**Statements**

| Subject | *have* | *(not)* | *been* | Base Form of Verb + *-ing* | |
|---|---|---|---|---|---|
| You | have | | been | doing | a great job. |
| He | has | not | been | following | instructions. |

**Grammar Note**

Use the present perfect continuous to talk about an action that started in the past and is still happening now.

**Yes/No Questions**

| *Have* | Subject | *been* | Base Form of Verb + *-ing* | |
|---|---|---|---|---|
| Has | she | been | asking | questions? |

**Short Answers**

| Yes, she **has**. | No, she **hasn't**. |
|---|---|

**Wh- Questions**

| *Wh-* Word | *have* | Subject | *been* | Base Form of Verb + *-ing* | |
|---|---|---|---|---|---|
| How long | have | they | been | working? | |

**Short Answers**

| Six months. |
|---|
| For about a year. |

### PRACTICE

**A** Complete the sentences with the present perfect continuous form of the verbs.

1. Performance evaluations _____ *have been changing* _____ for nurses.
<br>                                   change

2. Managers _____ to make the evaluations more objective.
<br>                    try

3. Susan _____ very hard lately.
<br>               work

4. She _____ about becoming an RN.
<br>            think

**B** Complete the conversations with the present perfect continuous form of the verbs.

1. **A:** _____ *Have you been thinking* _____ about your goals here?
<br>                    you / think

   **B:** Yes, _____ *I have* _____. I'd like to become a supervisor.

2. **A:** _____ long for his appointment?
<br>               he / wait

   **B:** Yes. _____ here for an hour!
<br>                   He / sit

3. **A:** How long _____ at this school?
<br>                         you / study

   **B:** One year, but _____ English since I was eight years old.
<br>                              I / learn

### WHAT ABOUT YOU?

**GROUPS OF 3** Talk about things you are doing now that started in the past.
Use the present perfect continuous.

## Write about your goals

**GET READY**

Susan is completing her performance evaluation form. She is writing about her goals.
Do you set goals for yourself at work or school?

**STUDY THE MODEL**

**A** Read the performance evaluation form. What is Susan's long-term goal?

 **Park View Hospital**

### PERFORMANCE EVALUATION FORM

**EMPLOYEE GOALS**

**Current Year Goals**

List at least 3 goals for this year and the specific steps you will take to reach those goals.

1. I will maintain a professional distance with my patients. To do this I will discuss my time limitations with patients. And I will make sure each patient gets equal attention.
2. I will increase my knowledge of the patient database. I plan to schedule a training session with the IT department, and I will spend at least 15 minutes each day working on the database.
3. I will improve and update my general nursing skills. I will attend at least 4 of the monthly training sessions offered by the department. I will also attend one of the nursing conventions at the Medical Center.
4. I will keep a record of my achievements and identify ways to improve my work performance. I will start a nursing journal this year and write in it once a week.

**Long-Term Goals**

List 1 goal that you want to reach in the next 5 years.

My long-term goal is to become a Registered Nurse within 4 years. This year I will start taking steps towards that goal. I will meet with the Human Resources department to get information about Park View's LVN-to-RN program.

---

**Writing Tip**

When writing about goals, it's important to use **quantifiable** language. Use numbers to say exactly what you want to do. Give dates or times for when you want to complete any actions. This will help you measure your success in achieving your goals.

---

**B** Read the Writing Tip. Then read the evaluation form again.
Underline 3 numbers that Susan used to quantify her goals.

**c** **Look at the chart Susan used to plan her evaluation, and complete it.**

| Goals | Steps Needed to Reach Goal |
|---|---|
| 1. work on maintaining professional distance | a. discuss _____ limitations with patients<br>b. spend an _____ amount of time with each patient |
| 2. increase knowledge of database | a. schedule a _____ session with IT<br>b. spend 15 min. every day working on database |
| 3. improve / update general nursing skills | a. attend 4 monthly training sessions<br>b. attend a convention at Medical Center |
| 4. keep a record of my achievements and ways to improve | a. start a _____ journal<br>b. write in it once a week |
| 5. (long-term) become an RN within 4 years | Meet with HR and get info about LVN-to-RN program |

## BEFORE YOU WRITE

You're going to list 4 short-term goals and 1 long-term goal, and then list the steps you will take to reach them. Complete the chart to plan your writing.

| Goals | Steps Needed to Reach Goal |
|---|---|
| 1. | |
| 2. | |
| 3. | |
| 4. | |
| 5. | |

## WRITE

Review the Model and the Writing Tip. Use the ideas from your chart to write about your goals and the steps you will take to reach them.

# LISTENING AND SPEAKING

## Ask about someone's belongings

**4**

### GET READY TO WATCH

Susan finds some things that people left at the nurses' station. Have you ever found an item that someone lost?

### WATCH

◼◀ **Watch the video. Read the statements. Circle *True* or *False*. Correct the false statements.**

| | | | |
|---|---|---|---|
| **1.** | The phone belongs to Ann. | True | False |
| **2.** | Ann knows who the glasses belong to. | True | False |
| **3.** | The sweater probably belongs to Jen. | True | False |
| **4.** | The watch belongs to Ann. | True | False |

### CONVERSATION

**A** ◼◀ **Watch part of the video. Complete the conversation.**

**Susan:** Hey, Ann. Is this your cell phone?

**Ann:** Nope. That isn't mine.

**Susan:** Maybe it's Sofia's. She was here a few

_____ ago.

**Ann:** Maybe. It does look like hers.

**Susan:** Oh, look at this! Someone left a pair of

_____, too. These aren't yours, by any chance?

**Ann:** No. I have no idea who those belong to.

**Susan:** Hmm. I guess I'll just put them under the counter.

**B** ◀))) **Listen and repeat.**

**C** PAIRS **Practice the conversation. Use your own names.**

**D** PAIRS **Make similar conversations. Talk about other objects in your classroom.**

> **Pronunciation Note**
>
> When we add -s to a word (for example, to make a plural noun or possessive), we pronounce the -s ending /s/, /z/, or /əz/. The pronunciation depends on the sound that comes before the -s ending.
>
> ◀))) **Listen and repeat.**
>
> | | | | |
> |---|---|---|---|
> | /s/ | minutes | looks | it's |
> | /z/ | Sofia's | hers | belongs |
> | /əz/ | glasses | watches | Mr. Sánchez's |

### WHAT DO YOU THINK?

GROUPS OF 3 What do you do if you find something someone lost? What items do you make an effort to return? When do you *not* make an effort to return something?

# GRAMMAR

## 5 Possessive pronouns

### STUDY Possessive pronouns

| Subject Pronoun | Possessive Adjective | Possessive Pronoun | Example |
|---|---|---|---|
| I | my | **mine** | That cell phone isn't **mine**. |
| you | your | **yours** | Is it **yours**? |
| he | his | **his** | Ask Jim. Maybe it's **his**. |
| she | her | **hers** | Pam was just here. Is this sweater **hers**? |
| we | our | **ours** | The red car is **ours**. |
| they | their | **theirs** | **Theirs** is the blue car. |

**Grammar Note**

Use possessive pronouns to answer questions beginning with *Whose*:
*Whose cell phone is this?*
You can also use possessive pronouns to clarify *Which one*:
*Which cup is yours? Mine is the one by the sink.*
When the possessive pronoun is the subject of the sentence, the verb that follows agrees with the omitted noun.

### PRACTICE

 **A** Complete the sentences. Circle the correct form.

1. **A:** Is this (your) / yours cell phone?
   **B:** No. Ask Angela. I think it's her / hers.
2. **A:** That's my / mine coat you picked up.
   **B:** Oh, sorry. I thought it was my / mine.
3. **A:** Her / Hers friends left early.
   **B:** Their / Theirs classes start in an hour.
4. **A:** Which one is our / ours bus?
   **B:** Our / Ours is over here, number 15.

**B** Rewrite each reply. Change the underlined words to possessive pronouns.

1. **A:** Did you leave these books in the classroom?
   **B:** No. Those aren't <u>my books</u>. <u>My books</u> have my name on them.

   > *B: No. Those aren't mine. Mine have my name on them.*

2. **A:** Is that Bill's umbrella? It looks the same as Mary's.
   **B:** Yes, it is <u>his umbrella</u>. <u>His umbrella</u> is dark green, and <u>her umbrella</u> is light green.
3. **A:** I like your artwork. It's really good.
   **B:** Thanks. <u>My artwork</u> is good, but I think <u>your artwork</u> looks better.
4. **A:** Oh, great! You brought cookies for the party! We did, too.
   **B:** <u>Our cookies</u> have chocolate chips. What flavor are <u>your cookies</u>?

## WHAT ABOUT YOU?

**GROUPS OF 4** Collect 3 items from each person in the group and put them together on a desk. Talk about who owns each item, using possessive pronouns.

## Complete a credit card application

### GET READY

Susan is completing an application to get a new credit card. Do you use credit cards? Do you have more than one?

### PRACTICAL READING

**A**  **Read the credit card application. What kind of information does Susan write on the application?**

---

**PARKDALE BANK**

**Credit Card Application Form**

Are you currently a customer with Parkdale Bank? _X_ Yes ____ No

Which credit card are you applying for?

_X_ No-Fee Card ____ Low APR Gold Card ____ Premium Rewards Card

**Contact Information**

SUSAN                          KIM                          08/27/1985
First name                  Last name                  Date of birth (MM/DD/YYYY)

1400 RICHMOND AVE.          HOUSTON, TX          77006
Street & House number      City, State              Zip code

(281) 555-3745              SUSAN.KIM@PARKVIEWMED.COM
Home phone                  Email

PARK VIEW HOSPITAL          LICENSED VOCATIONAL NURSE
Employer                    Occupation

1550 PARK RD., HOUSTON, TX 77004              (281) 555-8000
Employer address                              Business phone

**Financial Information**

Annual Income $ _35,360_____

How long have you lived at your current address? _1 YEAR_____

Do you own or rent your home? _RENT_____

| **Monthly Payments** | **Credit Card Debt** |
|---|---|
| $ _560_ Rent/mortgage | $ _590_ Credit Card 1—Existing Balance |
| $ _243_ Auto loan | $_____ Credit Card 2—Existing Balance |
| $_____ Other loan | $_____ Credit Card 3—Existing Balance |

Please add any other debt information on a separate piece of paper.

---

## B Read the application again. Answer the questions.

1. How many different types of cards can Susan apply for? _____

2. How much does Susan pay each month for rent? _____

3. What kind of loan does Susan have? _____

4. What is the amount of Susan's credit card debt right now? _____

## PRACTICAL LISTENING

### A ◀))) Look at the chart. Listen to a podcast about the different credit cards offered by Parkdale Bank. Complete the chart with the information you hear.

| Name of Card | Credit Limit | APR | Annual Fee | Benefits |
|---|---|---|---|---|
| No-Fee | _____ | 16.9% | $0 | none |
| Low APR Gold | $10,000 | 12.9% | $_____ | none |
| Premium Rewards | $12,000 | _____ | $99 | 1% rewards |

### B Look at the chart in Exercise A. Answer the questions.

1. Which card offers the lowest APR? _____

2. Which card has the highest annual fee? _____

3. Which card has the lowest credit limit? _____

## PRACTICAL SPEAKING

### A ◀))) A customer calls Parkdale Bank to get more information about the credit card offers. Listen and read.

**Agent:** Good morning. Parkdale Bank. How may I help you?

**Customer:** Hi. I want to apply for a credit card, and I have a question.

**Agent:** Certainly. I can help you with that.

**Customer:** I read that the Premium Rewards Card gives you 1% cash back. What does that mean, exactly?

**Agent:** It means that you get one dollar for every hundred dollars you spend.

**Customer:** You mean, the bank gives me money?

**Agent:** That's right. You can use your rewards points to get cash back. Or you can use your points to get store gift cards.

**Customer:** OK. I see. Thanks.

### B ◀))) Listen and repeat.

### C PAIRS Role play a conversation between a Parkdale Bank customer service agent and a customer. Ask and answer new questions about the Parkdale Bank credit cards.

## WHAT DO YOU THINK?

GROUPS OF 3 Imagine you want to apply for a credit card. Which Parkdale Bank credit card would be the best choice for you? Explain your answer.

# Identify cause and effect

## GET READY

Susan is reading an article about choosing a credit card. Have you ever received an offer to apply for a new credit card? What types of offers do credit card companies make to get new customers?

## READ

◀))) **Listen and read the article. What kind of advice does the article give?**

# Offers You <u>Can</u> Refuse

"Pay no interest for six months!" "Earn 5% cash back!" "Apply now and get $100!" Most of us have received credit card offers like these. Unfortunately, many of these offers are too good to be true. It's important to review any offer carefully, if you want to avoid making a costly mistake. Here are some common mistakes people make when choosing a credit card.

1. **Getting fooled by introductory rates.** Many customers are attracted by offers with interest rates as low as 0%. However, they don't realize that these low rates expire after a short period of time. "After six months, my rate changed from 0% to 39%!" says Gary G. "Suddenly I was paying these really high interest charges."

2. **Not reading the fine print.** The law requires credit card companies to give you the terms of their offers in writing. Usually these are in small print on the application. Not reading these details can get you into trouble. "I didn't realize that the card company charged a low-activity fee if I didn't use the card in 12 months," says Maria J. "I couldn't believe they could charge me for not using their card!"

3. **Not comparing APRs.** Credit card companies must state the interest rate they charge as an Annual Percentage Rate, or APR. You can save money if you look at many different offers and compare the rates. "I thought all cards were the same, so I didn't shop around," says Janelle P. "I could have gotten a much lower rate."

4. **Looking only at the rewards.** Many cards reward customers for purchases with cash back, airline tickets, or even donations to their favorite charity. Rewards are great, but be sure to consider all the terms of the offer. Reward cards frequently charge higher interest and fees. "My card paid 1% cash back," said Bob V. "But I was paying more in fees and interest than the value of my rewards!"

## AFTER YOU READ

### Reading Skill

A *cause* is the thing that makes something happen. An *effect* is a change that is caused by something. Events are often related by cause and effect—the first event is the cause and what follows is the effect. Being able to **identify cause-and-effect relationships** can help you understand the importance of different actions or events.

**Read the Reading Skill. Then read the article again. Find 3 events (causes) and what happens next (effects) when people do not review the credit card offers carefully.**

| | Cause | | Effect |
|---|---|---|---|
| **1.** | fooled by an introductory rate | → | pay high interest charges |
| **2.** | | → | |
| **3.** | | → | |
| **4.** | | → | |

## VOCABULARY STUDY  Adverbs with *-ly*

### Build Your Vocabulary

An adjective (a word that describes a noun) can often be changed to an **adverb** (a word that describes a verb) by adding *ly* to it. Note that not all words that end in *ly* are adverbs.

| Adjective | Example | Adverb | Example |
|---|---|---|---|
| slow | Jim is slow. | **slowly** | He walked slowly. |
| loud | The bell is loud. | **loudly** | The bell rang loudly. |
| clear | The instructions were clear. | **clearly** | The teacher spoke clearly. |

**Read the Build Your Vocabulary note. Then underline the verb in each sentence below. Complete the sentences with adjectives from the box. Use the adverb form.**

( careful    frequent    quick )

**1.** People _____ get credit card offers in the mail.

**2.** Rates on credit cards can rise _____ in a short time.

**3.** Review any credit card offer _____ before you sign an agreement.

## WHAT DO YOU THINK?

**GROUPS OF 3** What are the advantages and disadvantages of using a credit card? What are the advantages and disadvantages of paying in other ways?

**ON THE WEB**

For more information, go online and search "credit card mistakes." Find one new credit card mistake and report back to the class.

# 8

# LISTENING AND SPEAKING

## Talk about personal interests

oooooo ## GET READY TO WATCH

Susan and Ann are chatting at the end of their shift.
Guess: What do you think they are talking about?

## WATCH

**A** ◼◀ **Watch the video. Was your guess correct?**

**B** ◼◀ **Watch the video again. Circle the correct answers.**

1. Susan is going to _____ tonight.
   a. a movie theater          b. a club                c. a restaurant

2. Susan thinks that _____ is relaxing.
   a. having a quiet dinner    b. going out dancing     c. watching DVDs

3. Ann relaxes by _____.
   a. reading a book           b. going out with friends    c. watching late-night TV

## CONVERSATION

**A** ◼◀ **Watch part of the video. Complete the conversation.**

**Ann:**    Any plans for tonight?

**Susan:**  Yes. I'm going out _____ with some friends.
            A new club opened up downtown.

**Ann:**    Wow. Where do you get the energy? When I have an evening off,
            all I want to do is stay home and unwind.

**Susan:**  Oh, not me. Going out dancing is how I relax!
            It's a great way to blow off steam.

**Ann:**    Hmm. I'd probably be falling asleep on the dance floor.
            I'm always in bed by 10 o'clock.

**Susan:**  So, then, what do *you* do to _____?

**Ann:**    Me? I like to stay home and watch a movie or read a good book.
            Now *that's* the way to wind down.

**B** ◀))) **Listen and repeat.**

**C** **PAIRS** **Practice the conversation.**

**D** **PAIRS** **Make similar conversations. Talk about your plans for tonight or for the weekend.
Talk about how you like to relax.**

## WHAT DO YOU THINK?

**GROUPS OF 3** Do you think that physical exercise is helpful after a hard day at work?
What are some other ways to relieve stress and relax?

# JOB-SEEKING SKILLS
## Ask questions at a job interview

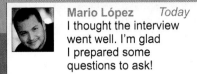

**Mario López**   *Today*
I thought the interview went well. I'm glad I prepared some questions to ask!

## GET READY

Mario continues his interview for the LVN position at Park View Hospital. What are some questions you might ask the interviewer at a job interview? Why is it a good idea to ask questions?

## ASK QUESTIONS AT A JOB INTERVIEW

**A** ◀)) **Listen to the second part of the interview. Check [✓] the questions that Mario asks.**

| Mario's Questions | The Interviewer's Answers |
|---|---|
| **1.** ☐ How would you describe the management style here? | |
| **2.** ☐ How will my performance be evaluated? | |
| **3.** ☐ Who is responsible for evaluating my performance? | |
| **4.** ☐ What are you looking for in your ideal candidate? | |
| **5.** ☐ Does the hospital provide support for advancement? | |
| **6.** ☐ What do you most enjoy about your work here? | |
| **7.** ☐ What are the challenges I would face here? | |
| **8.** ☐ Are there other job responsibilities not mentioned in the ad? | |
| **9.** ☐ May I contact you if I have further questions? | |
| **10.** ☐ When will you be making a decision? | |

**B** ◀)) **Listen again. What answers does the interviewer give to Mario's questions? Complete the chart.**

**C** **PAIRS** **Look again at the questions in the chart above. Discuss:**

1. Do you think it was a good idea for Mario to start by asking about the management style and performance evaluations? Why or why not?

2. Mario had already learned about the LVN-to-RN program, but he asked about support for advancement anyway. Do you think this was a good thing to do?

3. Do you think Mario should have asked any of the other questions from the chart? Which one(s)? Why?

## PUT YOUR IDEAS TO WORK

Write down the questions from the chart above that *you* would like to ask at a job interview. Can you think of other questions? Add them to your list. Then compare lists with a partner.

## GRAMMAR

In this unit, you studied:
- Present perfect continuous
- Possessive pronouns

See page 152 for your Grammar Review.

## VOCABULARY  See page 165 for the Unit 8 Vocabulary.

**Vocabulary Learning Strategy: Write Personal Sentences**

**A** Choose 10 words from the Unit 8 Word List. In your notebook, write sentences about yourself or your opinions on something with the words.

> I play soccer when I need to blow off steam. Kicking the ball helps me get rid of stress.

**B** Underline the vocabulary words in Exercise A.

## SPELLING  See page 165 for the Unit 8 Vocabulary.

**CLASS** Choose 10 words for a spelling test.

## LISTENING PLUS

**A** Watch each video. Write the story of Susan's day.

> Susan and Henry met to talk about Susan's work performance. Henry told Susan what she is doing well and also what she needs to improve.

**B** PAIRS Review the Lesson 8 conversation. See page 114. Role play the conversation for the class.

## NOW I CAN

**PAIRS** See page 103 for the Unit 8 Goals. Check ☑ the things you can do. Underline the things you want to study more. Tell your partner.

> I can _____. I need more practice with _____.

# 9 Alina Returns

## MY GOALS

- ☐ Talk about how to get a good deal
- ☐ Compare ways of buying things
- ☐ Read a return policy
- ☐ Talk about holiday plans
- ☐ Recognize illegal interview questions

Go to MyEnglishLab for more practice after each lesson.

**Alina Morales**

**Alina** *Today*
Lunch with my friend Nisrine today. Then I have to return some things I bought.

# LISTENING AND SPEAKING

## Talk about how to get a good deal

### GET READY TO WATCH

Nisrine is telling Alina about a good deal she got.
Have you ever gotten a really good deal at a store?

### WATCH

■◀ **Watch the video. Read the statements.**
**Circle *True* or *False*. Correct the false statements.**

1. Nisrine's watch was 50% off.                                    True    False
2. Alina wants Nisrine to send her a link to a store website.      True    False
3. Alina is worried about getting too many emails from stores.     True    False
4. Stores send coupons to Nisrine at a special email address.      True    False

### CONVERSATION

**A**  ■◀ **Watch part of the video. Complete the conversation.**

**Alina:**   How do you always find such great deals?

**Nisrine:**  I have my ways . . .

**Alina:**   OK . . . Like what?

**Nisrine:**  Well, one thing I do is subscribe to

_____ blogs.

**Alina:**   How does that work?

**Nisrine:**  Oh, it's easy. If you subscribe to one of these

blogs, you get email _____ with
news about sales and good deals.

**Alina:**   Nice.

**Nisrine:**  Yup. It's great because I don't have a lot of time to go online
looking for bargains. They do all the work for me!

> **Pronunciation Note**
>
> When we put two words together to
> make a compound noun, we usually
> put more stress on the first word.
>
> ◀))) **Listen and repeat.**
> **junk** mail            **news**letters
> **shop**ping blogs      **e**mail messages

**B**  ◀))) **Listen and repeat.**

**C**  PAIRS  **Practice the conversation.**

**D**  GROUPS OF 4  **What are some other ways you can get good shopping deals?**
**Write down your ideas.**

**E**  PAIRS  **Make similar conversations. Talk about ways of getting a good deal.**
**Use your ideas from Exercise D.**

### WHAT DO YOU THINK?

PAIRS  Do you think subscribing to shopping blogs is a good idea?
What could be some bad results of getting these messages?

# GRAMMAR

## Present real conditional

### STUDY  Present real conditional

| If Clause | Main Clause |
|---|---|
| If you go to this website, | you can find some good deals. |

| Main Clause | If Clause |
|---|---|
| Stores send you coupons | if you sign up for their newsletter. |

**Grammar Note**

Use the present real conditional to talk about general truths or scientific facts. You can also use the present real conditional to talk about habits or things that happen again and again.

Use an **imperative**, the **simple present**, or a **modal** (*can, might, should*) in the main clause.

Use the simple present in the *If* clause.

### PRACTICE

**A** **Combine the two sentences into one sentence using the present real conditional. Use a separate piece of paper.**

1. Nisrine buys something new. She always finds a good deal.

> If Nisrine buys something new, she always finds a good deal.

2. Alina signs up for the store newsletter. She can get coupons for some items.

3. She should get a separate email address. She doesn't want junk email messages.

4. You can save a lot of money. You know ways of shopping smart.

5. You shop at an online auction site. Make sure it is a good one.

6. You look at a comparison shopping website. You can compare prices at different stores.

**B** **Answer the questions on a separate piece of paper. Use the present real conditional and the phrases from the box.**

> ask friends for recommendations
> compare prices for different stores online
> find out what the return policy is
> check the product warranty
> ~~decide what model you want~~
> get your money back

1. You want to buy a new TV. What should you do first?

> If you want to buy a new TV, you should first decide what model you want.

2. You are not sure which model you want. What can you do?

3. You don't know how much TVs cost. What should you do?

4. You decide on a certain TV. What should you check before you buy it?

5. You think you are ready to buy.  What else should you find out?

6. You have a problem with your new TV, and you have your receipt. What might you be able to do?

### WHAT ABOUT YOU?

**PAIRS** Talk about your own shopping habits. Use the present real conditional.

*If I want to buy something, I usually wait until the store has a sale.*

Alina is reading an article about supermarket shopping. Check [✓] the things you do to prepare for a trip to the supermarket.

☐ read a sale circular      ☐ have a snack            ☐ make a shopping list
☐ find coupons             ☐ compare store prices    ☐ go to the store website

○○○○○○○ **READ**

◀)) **Listen and read the article. Why do shoppers need to be careful when shopping at a supermarket?**

# THE SAVVY SHOPPER

Teresa Villanueva is eating an apple and studying supermarket circulars. A professional shopper, she plans her store visits carefully. "The way to save money is to always have a plan," says Teresa. "First, find out what's on sale. Then make a list of what you need. Buy only the things on your list." Even Teresa's apple is part of the plan. "Before shopping, I eat a snack so that I'm not hungry in the store. Believe me, those candy bars in the checkout line are much harder to resist on an empty stomach!" According to Teresa, every part of a supermarket is designed to make you buy more than you need. We may call these practices "tricks," but stores call them "merchandising." To illustrate, here are a few more tricks that supermarkets don't want you to know about:

**Locating the floral and bakery departments near the entrance.** "It's no accident that you see flowers and smell baking bread when you enter the store," says Teresa. "These pleasant sensations put you in the mood to spend money."

**Keeping everyday items in the back of the store.** "How often have you gone into a store for an essential item such as bread, only to leave with a full bag of groceries? Stores know that customers will put more food in their baskets as they walk to the back of the store."

**Placing the most expensive items at eye level.** "People reach for products that are closer to their eyes and hands. If you want to save money, look on the bottom or top shelves. That's where the bargains are."

**5 for $5 sale pricing.** "Many shoppers don't realize they'll get the sale price even if they buy only one item. So they buy more than they need."

**Super-sizing the shopping carts.** "People tend to stop shopping when their cart is full. By increasing the cart size, supermarkets keep shoppers in the store."

## AFTER YOU READ

**Read the Reading Skill. Read the article again. Find and circle the signal words from the box. Then decide if the words show a sequence or a description and complete the chart.**

| first | then | before | to illustrate | such as |

| Sequence | Description |
|----------|-------------|
|          |             |
|          |             |
|          |             |

## VOCABULARY STUDY Context Clues

**Build Your Vocabulary**

One way to learn the meaning of an unknown word is to look at the **context**, or the words around it. These words can give you information, or **clues**, that will help you understand the meaning of the unknown word. Look for these **context clues**, and you will be able to guess the meaning of many new words.

| Context Clues | |
|---------------|--|
| **Type** | **Example** |
| synonym | Smart shoppers keep their impulses, or urges, under control. |
| definition | Stores use our impulses—sudden strong desires—to get us to buy more than we need. |
| example | Sue can't control her impulses. She sees something in a store and suddenly decides that she must buy it. |
| contrast | Tom controls his spending and only buys what he needs. Sue is the opposite. Her purchases are usually the result of impulses. |
| inference | Sue didn't plan to buy the scarf. She just had a sudden impulse. |

**Read the Build Your Vocabulary note. Find the words below in the article. Look for context clues that give information about the meaning of each word.**

| | Word | Context Clue |
|--|------|--------------|
| **1.** | floral | _____ |
| **2.** | bakery | _____ |
| **3.** | essential | _____ |
| **4.** | bargains | _____ |
| **5.** | super-sizing | _____ |

## WHAT DO YOU THINK?

**GROUPS OF 3** The goal of any business is to earn money. Do you think it is right for supermarkets to "trick" customers into buying more groceries than they need?

**ON THE WEB**

For more information, go online and search "supermarket shopping tips." Find a new tip and report back to the class.

### GET READY TO WATCH

Nisrine and Alina are talking about shopping online versus shopping in a store. Which kind of shopping do you prefer? Why?

### WATCH

◼◀ **Watch the video. Circle the correct words.**

1. Nisrine likes / doesn't like going to stores.

2. Nisrine thinks that the prices online / in a store are usually lower.

3. Alina prefers to buy clothes online / in a store.

4. Alina thinks it's easier to get information from a person / a computer.

5. Nisrine's daughter / sister knows a lot about computers.

### CONVERSATION

**A** ◼◀ **Watch part of the video. Complete the conversation.**

**Alina:** Nisrine, do you do a lot of your shopping on the Internet?

**Nisrine:** Oh, sure. Who wants to go to a store? The _____, the lines, the crowds . . . I prefer to just go online and shop from the comfort of my own home.

**Alina:** Yeah, I know what you mean. Shopping online is definitely more convenient than shopping in a real store.

**Nisrine:** And things are usually cheaper _____, too.

**Alina:** True. But for some things, I still prefer to go to a store.

**Nisrine:** Oh, yeah? For what?

**Alina:** Well, for _____, of course. You can't try on clothing if you're shopping online.

**B** ◀)) **Listen and repeat.**

**C** **PAIRS** **Practice the conversation. Use your own names.**

**D** **PAIRS** **What are some good and bad things about shopping online and shopping in a regular store? Write a list.**

**E** **SAME PAIRS** **Make similar conversations. Talk about whether you prefer to shop online or in a regular store. Use your ideas from Exercise D.**

---

**Pronunciation Note**

The words *the* and *to* have two pronunciations. Before a consonant sound, they have the short vowel /ə/. Before a vowel sound, they often have a clearer vowel sound: *the* /ði/ and *to* /tu/.

◀)) **Listen and repeat.**

the traffic, the lines, the crowds

on the Internet

to go

to a store

---

### WHAT DO YOU THINK?

**PAIRS** Shopping online has become so popular that some regular stores are going out of business. Do you think this is a problem? Why or why not?

### STUDY Comparatives

| Prices online are | (much) | **cheaper** | | prices in a store. |
|---|---|---|---|---|
| Shopping online is | (a lot) | **more convenient** | **than** | shopping in a store. |
| Store policies can be | | **less confusing** | | online policies. |

**Grammar Note**

If the thing you are comparing is known or has been
  mentioned, you can omit it: *Prices online are cheaper.*
For some adjectives, the spelling changes when *-er* is added:
*easy* → *easier*     *big* → *bigger*
*Good* and *bad* have irregular comparative forms: *better, worse.*

See page 161 for an explanation of spelling rules with comparative adjectives.

### PRACTICE

**A**  Complete the paragraphs with the comparative form of the adjectives.

Alina thinks going to a store is _____better_____ than shopping online for some
1. good

items. She says it's _____ to ask someone questions than to search for
2. easy

information online. Nisrine prefers shopping online because it's _____
3. fast

than going to a store and waiting in line. And the things she wants are usually

_____ online. Nisrine is _____ than Alina about
4. cheap                                      5. knowledgeable

shopping for bargains online.

**B**  Complete the paragraph with the adjectives from the box.
Use the comparative form and add *than* when necessary.

( close    convenient    expensive    friendly    ~~good~~    small )

Some people think that small local stores are (1.) ____better than____ large
mall stores. Local stores may be (2.) _____ to your home and therefore
(3.) _____ for you. Also, the owners in a small local store are often
(4.) _____ the people who work at a mall store. Of course, the selection of
items to choose from at a local store may be (5.) _____. And the items at
a large store are often (6.) _____ and can save you money.

### WHAT ABOUT YOU?

**PAIRS** Compare different types of stores. Talk about the prices, the quality of the products,
and other things that are important to you.

# 6

## Read a return policy

### GET READY

Alina buys a DVD online, but she needs to return it. When was the last time you returned something to a store?

### PRACTICAL READING

 **Read the return policy. What kind of a store is Alina's DVD from?**

**a.** an entertainment store    **b.** an electronics store    **c.** a department store

---

## PennyMart **Return Policy**

Home | Kids | Womens | Mens | About

You can return PennyMart merchandise either by mail or to a store. You can return most items within 90 days. Look at the chart for exceptions to this rule and for instructions on returning certain items.

All items must be returned in the original packaging. A receipt is required for all items.

| Type of Purchase | Return Policy |
| --- | --- |
| Books | Must be returned in new, unread condition. |
| Clothing, including footwear | Unworn, with the sales tags attached. |
| Electronics, including cameras, computers, computer software, GPS, electronic readers, video players | Must be returned within 15 days of purchase. |
| Gift cards | Not returnable. |
| Music and movies (DVDs and CDs) | Must be returned within 15 days of purchase. Return unopened only. |
| Plants | Do not return by mail. Please call Customer Service for assistance at 1-800-555-9876. |

---

 **Read the return policy again. Circle the correct words.**

**1.** Customers have 15 / 90 days to return most items.

**2.** Electronics / Plants must be returned within a shorter period of time.

**3.** A sales tag / receipt must be included with all returns.

**4.** Customers may not return gift cards / plants.

**5.** Books / Movies must be unopened.

**6.** Customers can't return clothing that is worn / opened.

**7.** Customers may not return plants / books by mail.

## PRACTICAL SPEAKING

**A** ◀)) **Alina's husband, Manuel, calls the customer service line to ask a question about returning the DVD. Listen and read.**

**Agent:** PennyMart Returns Department. Can I help you?

**Manuel:** Hi. Yes. I bought a DVD through your website, but it's damaged.

**Agent:** Oh. I'm sorry about that. Can you describe the damage?

**Manuel:** Well, the disc looks OK, but the picture doesn't show correctly.

**Agent:** I see. And when did you receive the DVD?

**Manuel:** Just this morning.

**Agent:** OK. In that case, you can exchange the DVD for the same title. Send it back in the original packaging and include the receipt. As soon as we receive it, we'll ship a new one to you.

**Manuel:** Thank you.

**B** ◀)) **Listen and repeat.**

**C** **PAIRS** **Role play a similar conversation. Ask new questions about items you need to return. Use items and information from the PennyMart return policy.**

## PRACTICAL LISTENING

◀)) **Listen to a podcast explaining what you need to check on return policies. Then read the statements. Circle *True* or *False*. Correct the false statements.**

| | | | |
|---|---|---|---|
| **1.** | Many stores post their return policy on their company website. | True | False |
| **2.** | All stores must give a customer at least 15 days to return an item. | True | False |
| **3.** | All stores will give you your money back when you return an item. | True | False |
| **4.** | If you buy an item online, you can sometimes return the item to a brick-and-mortar store instead of mailing it back. | True | False |
| **5.** | Some stores do not allow customers to return items that were on sale. | True | False |

## WHAT DO YOU THINK?

**GROUPS OF 3** Why is a clear return policy important for a store? How does it protect the rights of customers? Imagine that you owned a store. Write a return policy that is fair to both your store and to your customers.

**STORE RETURN POLICY**

_____

_____

_____

_____

# Write a letter of complaint

## GET READY

Alina is writing a letter of complaint about a product the hospital ordered. Have you ever written a letter of complaint?

## STUDY THE MODEL

**A** **Read the letter. What problem does Alina have with the product?**

🔆 **Park View Hospital**
1550 Park Rd., Houston, TX 77004 — Letterhead or sender's personal address

May 23, 2014 — Date

Mr. Charles Wright
Customer Services Manager
Nutrition for Life, Inc.
2230 Industrial Road
Houston, TX 77015

Re: Account # 715400820 — Subject line

Dear Mr. Wright: — Salutation

On April 20, 2014, Park View Hospital bought the nutrition analysis software *DietTrack* on the Nutrition for Life website. We received the software on April 27. A Nutrition for Life technician helped us to install the program on April 28.

Unfortunately, the *DietTrack* software does not work as well as I expected. I am disappointed because the program is missing important features. For example, the food database is incomplete. It does not have many of the common food items that our patients enjoy. I have to enter this information myself each time I use the program.

Since we are still within the 30-day trial period, we would like to receive a full refund for this purchase. I am enclosing a copy of the invoice. Please send instructions on how we can return the software.

Thank you for your help in resolving this matter. I look forward to your response. You can reach me at the hospital address above or call me directly at 1-281-555-2430.

Sincerely, — Closing

*Alina Morales*

Alina Morales
Clinical Dietitian — Typed name (and title)

**B** Read the Writing Tip. Then read the letter again. Label the *recipient address*, the *body*, and the *signature*.

**C** Read and complete the letter organizer Alina used to plan her letter.

---

**Paragraph 1: Description and history of purchase/service**

Bought nutrition analysis software on April 20 from
   Nutrition for Life website

Received it on _____

Technician helped install it on _____

---

**Paragraph 2: Description of the problem**

Product is not the same as advertised

Example: food _____ is incomplete—
   have to enter many common food items myself

---

**Paragraph 3: Action required/evidence enclosed**

Want full _____

Enclosing _____

---

**Paragraph 4: Thanks and contact information**

Can contact me at the hospital address or call
   me directly

---

## BEFORE YOU WRITE

**A** **PAIRS** Think of something you bought or a service you received that you were not happy about. Tell your partner what the problem was.

**B** You're going to write a letter of complaint about the product or service you described in Exercise A. Complete a letter organizer to plan your writing on a separate piece of paper.

## WRITE

Review the Model and the Writing Tip. Use the ideas from your letter organizer to write your letter of complaint.

# LISTENING AND SPEAKING

## Talk about holiday plans

### GET READY TO WATCH

Ida and Alina are looking forward to the Memorial Day holiday. What do you like to do on holidays or days off?

### WATCH

■◀ **Watch the video. Circle the correct answers.**

1. What is Ida going to do during the holiday?
   **a.** relax at home     **b.** go to the beach     **c.** have a barbecue

2. What is Alina going to do during the holiday?
   **a.** visit her relatives     **b.** go to the beach     **c.** have a barbecue

3. What do Ida and Alina want to do together during the summer?
   **a.** have a barbecue     **b.** play music     **c.** go to the beach

### CONVERSATION

**A**   ■◀ **Watch part of the video. Complete the conversation.**

**Ida:**     I'm so glad Memorial Day is coming up soon!

**Alina:**   That's right. Me, too. Are you doing anything special?

**Ida:**     I'm thinking about going to the _____ with my family.

**Alina:**   Oh, that sounds great.

**Ida:**     Yeah, I'm really looking forward to it. We'll have a picnic, go swimming . . . I can't wait!

**Alina:**   I'll bet.

**Ida:**     How about you? Do you have any plans for the _____?

**Alina:**   Oh, we always invite a bunch of people over and have a big barbecue. We'll just sit around all day and eat and talk.

**B**   ◀))) **Listen and repeat.**

**C**   PAIRS  **Practice the conversation.**

**D**   PAIRS  **Make similar conversations. Talk about your own holiday plans.**

## WHAT DO YOU THINK?

GROUPS OF 3  The U.S. observes ten public holidays per year—fewer than many other countries. What is the value of public or national holidays? Do you think the U.S. should observe more holidays? Why or why not?

# JOB-SEEKING SKILLS

## Recognize illegal interview questions

Mario López    *Today*
I want to be better prepared for my next job interview. I'm looking online for tips.

## GET READY

It is against the law for employers to ask certain types of questions in a job interview. What do you think are some questions that interviewers are not allowed to ask?

## RECOGNIZE ILLEGAL INTERVIEW QUESTIONS

**A** ◀)) **Mario is listening to a podcast about illegal interview questions. Listen to the podcast. What is the best way to answer an illegal interview question?**

☐ refuse to answer the question

☐ respond to the interviewer's concern

☐ explain that the question is illegal

**B** ◀)) **GROUPS OF 3 Listen to the podcast again. Check [✓] the questions that are illegal to ask in a job interview.**

☐ What is your date of birth?

☐ Are you over the age of 18?

☐ Where were your parents born?

☐ What country do you come from?

☐ Do you have any disabilities?

☐ Do you go to church on Sundays?

☐ Can you work on Sunday mornings?

☐ Are you planning to have children?

☐ Have you ever been injured on the job?

☐ What child-care arrangements have you made?

☐ Are you legally authorized to work in the U.S.?

☐ Are you physically able to lift boxes weighing 25 pounds?

## PUT YOUR IDEAS TO WORK

**A** **Read part of a job interview. Cross out the illegal interview question. Underline the sentence where the interviewee avoids the question. Circle the sentence where the interviewee responds to the interviewer's concern.**

**Interviewer:** Thanks for coming in today.

**Interviewee:** Of course. Thanks for calling me in to interview.

**Interviewer:** I love your accent. Where are you from?

**Interviewee:** Oh, I've moved around. But I'm legally authorized to work in the U.S.

**Interviewer:** That's good. Do you have any experience working in a warehouse?

**Interviewee:** Yes. I've worked for two years as a forklift driver.

**Interviewer:** Great. Did you receive forklift training certification at that job?

**Interviewee:** Yes, I did.

**B** **PAIRS Role play job interviews. Then change roles.**
**Student A:** You are a job interviewer. Ask an illegal question from Exercise B.
**Student B:** You are the interviewee. Avoid answering the illegal question, but respond to the interviewer's concern.

## GRAMMAR

In this unit, you studied:

- Present real conditional
- Comparatives

See page 153 for your Grammar Review.

## VOCABULARY  See page 166 for the Unit 9 Vocabulary.

**Vocabulary Learning Strategy: Group by Function**

**A** Complete each category with words from the Unit 9 Word List.

- shopping: ___bargain___, _____, _____,
  _____, _____, _____.
- leisure time: ___barbecue___, _____, _____,
  _____, _____, _____.
- personal characteristics: ___gender___, _____,
  _____, _____.

**B** Underline five words in Exercise A. Write a sentence with each word.

## SPELLING  See page 166 for the Unit 9 Vocabulary.

**CLASS** Choose 10 words for a spelling test.

## LISTENING PLUS

**A** Watch each video. Write the story of Alina's day.

Alina and Nisrine ate lunch together in the hospital cafeteria.
Nisrine gave Alina tips about how to get good shopping deals.

**B** **PAIRS** Review the Lesson 8 conversation. See page 128. Role play the conversation for the class.

## NOW I CAN

**PAIRS** See page 117 for the Unit 9 Goals.  Check ☑ the things you can do.
Underline the things you want to study more. Tell your partner.

> I can _____. I need more practice with _____.

# 10

# Henry Takes Steps

## MY GOALS

☐ Talk about getting ahead on the job

☐ Read a course catalog

☐ Talk about someone I admire

☐ Talk about long-term goals

☐ Respond to a job offer

Go to MyEnglishLab for more practice after each lesson.

**Henry Keita**
Henry          *Today*
I'm going to meet with my manager, Sueli. We're going to talk about advancing my career.

131

# LISTENING AND SPEAKING

## Talk about getting ahead on the job

### GET READY TO WATCH

Henry is talking to his manager, Sueli, about ways to advance his career. What are some ways you know for people to get ahead on the job?

### WATCH

◼◀ **Watch the video. Read the statements. Circle *True* or *False*. Correct the false statements.**

| | | |
|---|---|---|
| **1.** Henry wants to take on more responsibility at the hospital. | True | False |
| **2.** Sueli offers Henry a promotion. | True | False |
| **3.** Henry wants to spend less time with patients. | True | False |

### CONVERSATION

 ◼◀ **Watch part of the video. Complete the conversation.**

**Sueli:** Have you ever thought about becoming a nurse practitioner?

**Henry:** Well, I've thought about it. But I'd need more _____ for that.

**Sueli:** True. If you want to take that path, you'll need to get a master's degree.

**Henry:** Hmm. The problem is, I can't afford to stop working.

**Sueli:** Well, most schools have a part-time _____. And, you know, Park View does have a tuition reimbursement program.

**Henry:** I know. Well, maybe it's something I should think more about.

**Sueli:** I suggest you speak to Pam in Human Resources. She can give you information

about some _____ programs as well as how the tuition reimbursement works.

**Henry:** OK. I'll do that.

**B** ◀)) **Listen and repeat.**

**C** **PAIRS** **Practice the conversation.**

**D** **PAIRS** **What steps do you need to take to get a promotion at your job?**

**E** **SAME PAIRS** **Role play a conversation between a manager and an employee. Talk about a possible promotion and the steps needed to achieve that goal. Use your ideas from Exercise D.**

> ### Pronunciation Note
>
> Notice the stress in these words. Notice that in words with *-tion* or *-sion*, we usually stress the syllable just before *-tion* or *-sion*.
>
> ◀)) **Listen and repeat.**
>
> un·der·**stand**          ap·**pre**·ci·ate
> re·im·**burse**·ment      re·spon·si·**bil**·i·ty
> tu·**i**·tion             in·for·**ma**·tion
> de·**ci**·sion            prac·**ti**·tion·er

### WHAT DO YOU THINK?

**GROUPS OF 3** In the video, Henry doesn't accept the promotion that Sueli offers. Do you think this is a good decision? Explain your answer.

**STUDY** Future real conditionals

| If Clause | Result Clause |
| --- | --- |
| If you get a master's degree, | you **will** have more career options. |
| If Henry accepts the promotion, | he **might not** be happy. |

| Result Clause | If Clause |
| --- | --- |
| Henry **might** learn new skills | if he takes the promotion. |
| I **won't** take classes | if I can't study part-time. |

**Grammar Note**

Use the future real conditional to talk about what you think
will happen in the future based on action you take now.
Use the simple present in the *If* clause.
Use *will* or *might* in the result clause.

## PRACTICE

**A** **Circle the correct forms.**

1. If Henry (takes) / will take the promotion, more nurses will report to him.

2. If he has / will have more administrative duties, he won't see patients as often.

3. Henry thinks if he takes the job, it doesn't make / won't make him happy.

4. If Henry gets / will get a master's degree, he might be able to advance his career.

5. Henry will need to find a part-time program if he wants / will want to keep working.

**B** **Complete the sentences with the correct form of the verbs.
More than one answer may be possible.**

1. If you _____*get*_____ a post-secondary degree, you _____*will earn*_____ more money.
   <br>           get                          earn

2. If the weather _____ nice next Saturday, we _____ to the park.
   <br>                      be                              go

3. Petra _____ you up if you _____ a ride tonight.
   <br>             pick                   not have

4. I _____ you later if we _____ some help.
   <br>           call                 need

5. The supervisor _____ everyone know if we _____ next Friday off.
   <br>            let                have

6. If your work _____ finished, you _____ to stay late.
   <br>        be not                have

## WHAT ABOUT YOU?

**PAIRS** Talk about what you will or might do in different future situations.
Use the future real conditional.

## Read a course catalog

### GET READY

Henry is looking at a course catalog for a college nursing program. What kind of information do you think a course catalog includes?

### PRACTICAL READING

**A** Read the page from a college course catalog. Was your answer correct?

---

**School of Nursing**
**Course Descriptions**

**Core Courses**

**MN2501 Nursing Theory**      **2 CR LECT**
Nursing theory describes the goals, roles, and functions of nursing. In this course, you will learn the purpose of theory. You will see how nursing theory developed and will be introduced to the main theories of nursing. You will be encouraged to apply these theories to your own professional experiences.
Prerequisite: None

**MN2705 Information Systems in Nursing**      **3 CR LAB**
Information systems are computer systems that help manage data such as patient charts and staff schedules more efficiently. You will learn how to use these tools to improve patient care in different health care settings.
Prerequisite: None

**MN3100 Statistics in Nursing**      **2 CR LECT**
This course focuses on the value and use of statistics and statistical methods in health care research. You will learn how to collect, analyze, and interpret numerical data.
Prerequisite: None

**MN6120 Medical History and Physical Exam**      **3 CR LECT / CLIN**
This course will prepare you to assess patients' health at different stages of life, from birth through old age. You will collect data from a patient's medical history and will perform a physical examination. You will develop critical-thinking and decision-making skills.
Prerequisite: None

**MN7000 Thesis I**      **4 CR**
This course explains the basic requirements for writing a thesis. You will discuss ideas for a thesis topic and develop a thesis proposal. After completing this course, you will continue to develop your proposal in Thesis II.
Prerequisites: MN2501, MN3100

---

**B** Read the course catalog again. Read the statements.
Circle *True* or *False*. Correct the false statements.

1. The course number for *Nursing Theory* is MN6120.     True     False

2. Students can earn two credits for completing the *Statistics in Nursing* course.     True     False

3. The *Information Systems in Nursing* course involves working in a computer lab.     True     False

4. The *Medical History and Physical Exam* course involves working in a clinic with patients.     True     False

5. Students must complete two other courses before enrolling in *Thesis I*.     True     False

6. Students must complete the *Nursing Theory* course before they can enroll in the *Statistics in Nursing* course.     True     False

7. The course *Statistics in Nursing* will teach students how to give a physical examination.     True     False

8. In the course *Information Systems in Nursing*, students learn how to manage patient information using a computer system.     True     False

## PRACTICAL LISTENING

 Henry is listening to a podcast with information about course catalogs. Listen and answer the questions.

1. What are core courses?
   a. courses that you have to take in order to graduate
   b. courses that match your schedule and interests
   c. all the courses in your program of study

2. What is a prerequisite?
   a. a statistics course
   b. a class that you must take in order to graduate
   c. a class that you must take first, before you can take a second class

3. What is one resource students can use to help plan their classes?
   a. an academic advisor
   b. school policies
   c. a registration manager

4. What topics should students talk to their academic advisor about?
   a. homework assignments
   b. the courses the students need to take
   c. test dates

## WHAT DO YOU THINK?

**PAIRS** A course catalog is one source of information about the courses that are offered at a school. What are some other ways you can learn about these courses?

# LISTENING AND SPEAKING

## 4 Talk about someone you admire

### GET READY TO WATCH

Henry and Rick are talking about a doctor they admire. What personal characteristics do you think make someone a good manager or employee?

### WATCH

■◀ **Watch the video. Circle the correct answers.**

1. Henry and Rick admire Dr. Helms's _____.
   - **a.** patience
   - **b.** good judgment
   - **c.** enthusiasm

2. In stressful situations, Dr. Helms _____.
   - **a.** stays calm
   - **b.** asks for help
   - **c.** gets nervous

3. Henry talks about Dr. Peters as an example of someone who _____.
   - **a.** makes quick decisions
   - **b.** deals well with stress
   - **c.** changed with experience

### CONVERSATION

**A** ■◀ **Watch part of the video. Complete the conversation.**

**Henry:** Dr. Helms is great. I think she's the smartest _____ I've ever worked with. It's amazing how good she is at diagnosing patients.

**Rick:** Yeah, it really is. I mean, people come into the ER with all kinds of health conditions. It's not easy to figure out what's wrong.

**Henry:** True. That takes more than just knowledge. It takes good judgment, too.

**Rick:** And you have to be able to make _____ decisions. Not every doctor can do that.

**Henry:** I know. And Dr. Helms always stays

_____ under pressure, even when she's making life-or-death decisions.

**Rick:** Right. I don't know how she does it.

**B** ◀))) **Listen and repeat.**

**C** PAIRS **Practice the conversation.**

**D** PAIRS **Practice the conversation again. Make similar conversations. Talk about someone you admire. Describe his or her personal characteristics.**

---

**Pronunciation Note**

Many English words begin with groups of two or three consonant sounds. Say the consonants closely together.

◀))) **Listen and repeat.**

She's the smartest doctor.

She stays calm under pressure.

It's a stressful place.

---

### WHAT DO YOU THINK?

PAIRS In the video, Henry and Rick agree that people's personal characteristics can change over time. Do you agree? Or do you think people mostly stay the same during their lives?

---

# GRAMMAR

## 5 Superlatives

### STUDY Superlatives

| Dr. Helms is | **the smartest** | doctor in the ER. |
|---|---|---|
| She is | **the most capable** | doctor. |
| Data entry is | **the least exciting** | part of Henry's job. |

**One of + Superlative**

| He is | **one of** | **the most interesting** | people | I know. |
|---|---|---|---|---|
| She is | **one of** | **the best** | doctors | I've worked with. |

See page 161 for an explanation of spelling rules with superlative adjectives.

> **Grammar Note**
>
> For some adjectives, the spelling changes when *-est* is added:
> *easy* ⟶ *easiest*
> *big* ⟶ *biggest*
> *Good* and *bad* have irregular superlative forms: *best, worst*.

### PRACTICE

**A** Complete the sentences with the correct form of the adjectives.

1. Henry thinks that the ER is _____the most interesting_____ department in the hospital.
   <small>interesting</small>

2. Rick is Henry's _____ friend.
   <small>close</small>

3. Of all of Henry's friends, Rick gives Henry _____ advice.
   <small>good</small>

4. Rick thinks that the ER is _____ place to work in the hospital.
   <small>stressful</small>

5. Henry's decision to become a nurse practitioner is one of _____
   <small>hard</small>
   decisions he will ever make.

6. Henry thinks that Rick is _____ person to talk to for career advice.
   <small>helpful</small>

**B** Complete the sentences with the adjectives from the box. Use the superlative form.

> big    dependable    early    ~~good~~    happy    young

1. _____The best_____ decision Phil ever made was to get a degree. Now he makes a lot more money than he used to.

2. _____ mistake Janela ever made was moving to a new apartment. Her rent is higher, and her commute is longer.

3. Maria likes to take _____ bus to work so she can be there first in the morning.

4. Melissa has three children. Her _____ child is still a baby.

5. _____ day of Dan's life was his wedding day. He and his wife have been married for 20 years.

6. I can always count on Carla to help me. She is _____ person that I know.

### WHAT ABOUT YOU?

**PAIRS** Talk about events in your life and people you know. Use superlative adjectives.

# 6 Write a personal narrative

## GET READY

Henry is sending a message to an old friend on a social networking website. Have you ever met a friend that you had not seen in a long time? What did you talk about?

## STUDY THE MODEL

**A** Read Henry's message. What news about his life does he write about?

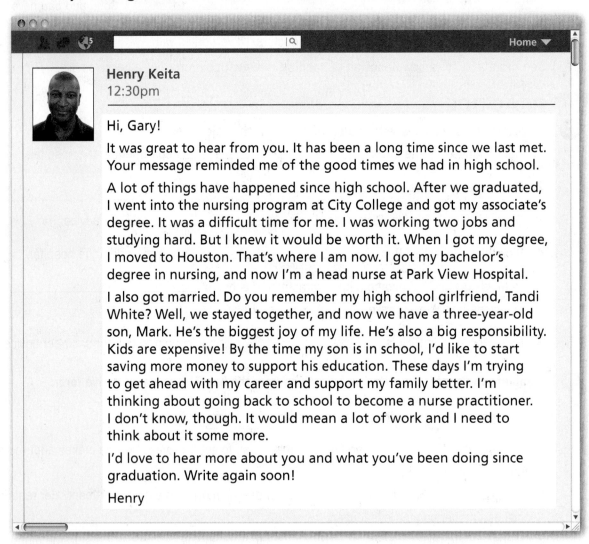

**Henry Keita**
12:30pm

Hi, Gary!

It was great to hear from you. It has been a long time since we last met. Your message reminded me of the good times we had in high school.

A lot of things have happened since high school. After we graduated, I went into the nursing program at City College and got my associate's degree. It was a difficult time for me. I was working two jobs and studying hard. But I knew it would be worth it. When I got my degree, I moved to Houston. That's where I am now. I got my bachelor's degree in nursing, and now I'm a head nurse at Park View Hospital.

I also got married. Do you remember my high school girlfriend, Tandi White? Well, we stayed together, and now we have a three-year-old son, Mark. He's the biggest joy of my life. He's also a big responsibility. Kids are expensive! By the time my son is in school, I'd like to start saving more money to support his education. These days I'm trying to get ahead with my career and support my family better. I'm thinking about going back to school to become a nurse practitioner. I don't know, though. It would mean a lot of work and I need to think about it some more.

I'd love to hear more about you and what you've been doing since graduation. Write again soon!

Henry

### Writing Tip

When writing a personal narrative, use **adverbial clauses of time** such as *After I graduated* or *When I moved* to show how events are connected. Remember to use commas when these clauses come at the beginning or in the middle of the sentence.

**B** Read the Writing Tip. Then read Henry's message again. Underline 3 adverbial clauses of time.

**C** Look at the diagram Henry used to plan his message, and complete it.

| Past | Present | Future |
|---|---|---|
| **Career**<br>• went to _____ for nursing<br>• got associate's degree<br>• moved to _____<br>• got bachelor's degree<br><br>**Personal**<br>• married _____ | **Career**<br>• still live in Houston<br>• work as the _____ at Park View Hospital<br><br>**Personal**<br>• have a three-year-old _____ named Mark | **Career**<br>• thinking about going back to school to become a _____<br>• want to earn more to support family<br><br>**Personal**<br>• want to save money for Mark's _____ |

## BEFORE YOU WRITE

You're going to write a message about your life to an old friend.
Think about important events in your life, what you are doing now,
and your plans for the future. Complete the diagram to plan your message.

| Past | Present | Future |
|---|---|---|
| Career<br><br><br>Personal | Career<br><br><br>Personal | Career<br><br><br>Personal |

## WRITE

Review the Model and the Writing Tip. Use the ideas from your diagram
to write your message.

## GET READY

Henry is reading an online article about the value of a college education.
Guess: What percent of jobs require a two- or four-year college degree?

☐ 75%  ☐ 40%  ☐ 20%

## READ

🔊)) **Listen and read the article. Was your guess correct?**

# Is College Worth It?

We asked two experts whether a two- or four-year college degree is still worth the investment. Here are their arguments:

### Education Brings Many Advantages

*Dr. Diego E. Gonzalez, Director of the National Center on Education and the Workforce*

I believe that a college education is a good idea for many reasons. With a degree, you'll earn more money. According to the Bureau of Labor Statistics, a worker with a bachelor's degree can make 40% more money than a worker with only a high school diploma. You'll also have an easier time finding a job. The National Governors' Association predicts that by 2014, 75% of jobs will require a two- or four-year degree.

However, an education brings much more than just financial rewards. It's a chance for self-improvement. In earning a degree, you'll gain knowledge and skills. You'll learn to think critically. And you'll develop strong work habits and self-confidence.

Finally, in earning a degree, you'll develop a network of friends within your career field. These are people that you can turn to when you need help.

A college degree will give you clear advantages in life. Give yourself this opportunity.

### College Isn't Always a Good Investment

*Susan F. Jacobsen, author of "Rip Off U: Why College Doesn't Pay"*

A college degree is not right for everyone. College is expensive. According to the College Board, the average cost of a public, four-year college is $20,100 per year. The cost of a public, two-year college is $12,398. For most students, this means taking out loans, which must be repaid after graduation. Often the jobs that you can get with these degrees don't pay enough to justify the investment.

Two to four years is a big investment in time. For many careers, this time could be better spent working. Instead of sitting in a classroom, you could be earning money and gaining job skills and experience.

Many people have been highly successful without earning a degree. Look at Apple CEO Steve Jobs and Facebook founder Mark Zuckerberg. Both men are college dropouts.

Talent and hard work are the real keys to success. Find your own path!

## AFTER YOU READ

### Reading Skill

A **fact** is a piece of information that is true. An **opinion** is a personal idea about something. Learning to identify facts and opinions in an article will help you understand the author's ideas and become a critical thinker.

**A** **Read the Reading Skill. Read the article again. Then read the statements from the article. Circle *Fact* or *Opinion*.**

1. I believe that a college degree is a good idea for many reasons.     Fact     Opinion

2. A college degree is not right for everyone.     Fact     Opinion

3. According to the College Board, the average cost of a public, four-year college is $20,100 per year.     Fact     Opinion

**B** **Look at the average earnings chart. Answer the questions.**

1. What is the average pay per week for a person with a bachelor's degree?

2. Which degree earned an average pay of $768 per week?

3. Which degree paid the highest average pay per week?

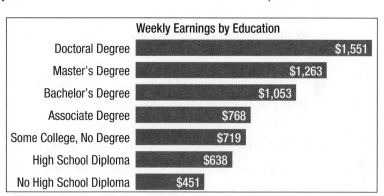

Weekly Earnings by Education

| | |
|---|---|
| Doctoral Degree | $1,551 |
| Master's Degree | $1,263 |
| Bachelor's Degree | $1,053 |
| Associate Degree | $768 |
| Some College, No Degree | $719 |
| High School Diploma | $638 |
| No High School Diploma | $451 |

## VOCABULARY STUDY  Word Families

### Build Your Vocabulary

A **word family** is a group of words that have the same root word—the part of the word that contains its basic meaning. Learning the meaning of the root can help you figure out the meaning of other words in that word family.

| Word Families | | |
|---|---|---|
| **Root** | **Meaning** | **Example** |
| -cess | to go | access, necessity, excessively, |
| kno- | to know, skill | know, acknowledge, |
| -dict | to say | dictate, diction, contradiction, |

**Read the Build Your Vocabulary note. Then read the article again.**
**Find a word from each word family and add it to the chart.**

## WHAT DO YOU THINK?

**GROUPS OF 3** Do you think that a two- or four-year degree is worth the time and money? Explain your opinion. Give facts to support your answer.

**ON THE WEB**

For more information, go online and search "value of a college education." Find one fact and report back to the class.

# Talk about long-term goals

 ## GET READY TO WATCH

Henry is talking to Rick about his goals.
Do you have long-term goals? Who do you
talk to about your goals?

 ## WATCH

◼◀ **Watch the video. Answer the questions.**

**1.** What did Henry do during his lunch break?

_____

**2.** What three things does Rick mention would be difficult about a degree program?

_____

**3.** What is Rick's advice to Henry? _____

**4.** What does Rick say Henry can do with him? _____

## CONVERSATION

Ⓐ ◼◀ **Watch part of the video. Complete the conversation.**

**Henry:** I've been looking into going back to school, maybe completing a
nurse practitioner program.

**Rick:** Oh, wow. That would open up a lot of possibilities for you.

**Henry:** Definitely. And it would also boost my _____.
Now that I have a son, I have to think about that.

**Rick:** Of course. So have you started looking into programs?

**Henry:** A little bit. I was doing some online _____ during my lunch break.

**Rick:** That's great. A nurse practitioner. You know, I could really see you doing that.

Ⓑ  **Listen and repeat.**

Ⓒ PAIRS **Practice the conversation.**

Ⓓ PAIRS **Talk about one of your own long-term goals. What steps must you take to achieve
that goal? What would be the benefits of achieving it?**

Ⓔ SAME PAIRS **Make similar conversations. Talk about your own goals.
Use your ideas from Exercise D.**

## WHAT DO YOU THINK?

PAIRS In the video, Rick tells Henry to take things "one step at a time."
What does this mean? Do you agree with this advice?

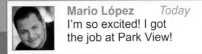

Mario López    Today
I'm so excited! I got the job at Park View!

## GET READY

The HR manager at Park View Hospital offers Mario a nursing position. When was the last time someone offered you a job? What did you talk about during that conversation?

## RESPOND TO A JOB OFFER

**A** ◀)) **Listen to the phone conversation. What kind of information does the HR manager give Mario?**

**B** ◀)) **Listen to the conversation again and complete Mario's notes.**

First Day of Work

May _____ at

_____ A.M.

First Day Schedule

9:00: meet with HR / fill in

_____

10:00: _____

Afternoon: _____

_____

**C** ◀)) **Listen and read part of the conversation.**

**Angela:** Good afternoon, Mr. López. This is Angela Pasco from the Human Resources department at Park View Hospital.

**Mario:** Oh, yes. Hi.

**Angela:** I'm calling about the LVN position you interviewed for. We're really excited to offer you the job. We think you'll make a great addition to our nursing staff.

**Mario:** That's great!

**Angela:** Now, this is a full-time position on the 8:00 A.M. to 4:30 P.M. shift.

**Mario:** OK.

**Angela:** We can offer you the hourly wage that we discussed earlier. We also provide full benefits including health insurance and a dental and vision plan.

**Mario:** That sounds fine. I'd be happy to accept your offer.

**D** ◀)) **Listen and repeat.**

**E** PAIRS **Practice the conversation.**

## PUT YOUR IDEAS TO WORK

**A** PAIRS **Talk about your dream job. What type of schedule, wages, and benefits would you like to have?**

**B** SAME PAIRS **Role play a new conversation between an HR manager and a job-seeker. Then change roles.**
**Student A:** Offer your partner his or her dream job.
**Student B:** Respond to the offer. Use your ideas from Exercise A.

## GRAMMAR

In this unit, you studied:

- Future real conditionals
- Superlatives

See page 154 for your Grammar Review.

## VOCABULARY  See page 166 for the Unit 10 Vocabulary.

### Vocabulary Learning Strategy: Write a Short Story

**A** Choose 5 to 10 words from the Unit 10 Word List. In your notebook, write a short story with the words.

> Jane had worked as a secretary in the science department of a large
> university for thirty years. She was a very capable secretary, but
> she dreamed of one day becoming a scientist . . .

**B** Underline the vocabulary words in Exercise A.

## SPELLING  See page 166 for the Unit 10 Vocabulary.

CLASS  Choose 10 words for a spelling test.

## LISTENING PLUS

**A** Watch each video. Write the story of Henry's day.

> Henry asked Sueli for advice about how to advance his career at the hospital.
> Sueli told Henry that she was thinking of offering him a promotion.

**B** PAIRS  Review the Lesson 4 conversation. See page 136. Role play the conversation for the class.

## NOW I CAN

PAIRS  See page 131 for the Unit 10 Goals.  Check ☑ the things you can do. Underline the things you want to study more. Tell your partner.

> I can _____. I need more practice with _____.

## ADVERBS OF FREQUENCY

**Look at the chart. How do you get to school? Complete the chart with your own information. Then complete the sentences. More than one answer may be possible.**

**Ways of Getting to School**
S = Stefano      P = Pilar      _____ = You

|  | Always | Usually | Often | Sometimes | Never |
|---|---|---|---|---|---|
| walk |  |  |  |  | S, P |
| take the bus/train |  |  |  | P | S |
| drive | S |  |  |  | P |
| ride a bicycle |  | P |  |  | S |

1. Stefano _never rides a bicycle to school_____.
2. Stefano and Pilar _____.
3. Pilar _____.
4. Stefano _____.
5. Pilar _____.
6. Stefano _____.
7. I _____.
8. I _____.

## QUANTIFIERS

**Complete the paragraph. Circle the correct quantifiers.**

Tanya's daughter, Sashi, is sick with the flu. Sashi felt OK this morning, but she began to feel sick when she got to school. The school nurse said that (1.) many / much of the children are out sick today. Tanya had to leave work early to pick up Sashi. (2.) Most / Many of the time, Tanya's parents are available to pick Sashi up from school, but today they were busy. Tanya hopes that her parents can take care of Sashi tomorrow. (3.) Both / A couple of her parents are retired, and they live nearby. Tanya's son, Anton, is in daycare. Luckily, Anton isn't sick. However, (4.) several / much of the children in his class are sick. And (5.) some / a little of the teachers have the flu now, too. The school nurse gave Tanya (6.) several / a lot of information about taking care of the children during the flu season. She said that Tanya needs to drink (7.) lots / each of fluids and get plenty of rest.

## FUTURE FORMS

**Complete the conversation with the correct future form of the verb.**
**More than one answer may be possible.**

**A:** Have you made your travel plans yet?

**B:** Yes, Barbara and I (1. fly) _____ are flying _____ to New York tomorrow afternoon.

**A:** Oh. So soon? Then I think I (2. cancel) _____ the barbecue for this weekend.

I (3. reschedule) _____ it for next week, when you get back.

**B:** Great. Thanks.

**A:** Don't forget to pack an umbrella.

**B:** Actually, I just checked the weather forecast. It (4. not / rain) _____.

**A:** Well, be sure to call me when you arrive. You know how I worry.

**B:** I know, Mom. But everything (5. be) _____ fine. New York is actually a very safe city.

Please don't worry. I (6. call) _____ you when I arrive at the hotel. I promise!

**A:** OK. But I know I (7. worry) _____ about you anyway. It's my job—I'm your mother!

## PAST ABILITY WITH *BE ABLE TO* AND *COULD*

**Read the paragraph. Write 5 sentences about what Jessica and her family could do and 5 sentences about what they were not able to do.**

My Unusual Childhood

By Jessica

When I was seven years old, my family moved to a cabin in Wisconsin. At first, life in the cabin was difficult. I was bored. We didn't have electricity, so there was no TV. I missed watching my favorite TV shows. Also, we lived far from any towns. There were no shopping malls or movie theaters. I missed playing with my old friends. My parents had to work hard. My mother was good at gardening and grew lots of fruit and vegetables. My father raised a few animals: chickens, rabbits, and two goats. He thought he would raise them for food, but he loved animals too much. We kept them as pets, instead. My father learned to make cheese from the goats' milk and get eggs from the chickens. After a while, I started to enjoy our new life. In the winter, I went skiing. In the summer, we went swimming in a nearby river. I spent hours exploring the woods and climbing trees. As I look back on my unusual childhood, our cabin was a great place to grow up.

# GRAMMAR REVIEW

## USED TO

Look at the chart about Delia and John. Write 5 sentences about the things they used to and didn't use to do. Use *used to* and *didn't use to*.

| Activity | Delia | | John | |
|---|---|---|---|---|
| | Then | Now | Then | Now |
| go out dancing | X | | X | |
| watch DVDs | | X | | X |
| sleep late on Saturday mornings | | | X | |
| cook dinner once a week | | | | X |
| exercise three times a week | X | | | |
| wear jeans every day | | X | | |

Delia and John used to go out dancing.

## PAST CONTINUOUS

Talia and Marta are talking about a big storm. Complete their conversation with the past continuous form of the verbs.

**Talia:** Can you believe the storm we had yesterday?

**Marta:** I know. It was crazy! What ___were you doing___ when it hit?
1. do

**Talia:** I was at home. Diego and I _____ just _____.
2. relax

I _____ about going out to the store for some groceries.
3. think

Diego _____ television, so luckily he heard the news that the storm
4. watch

_____. We closed all the windows and stayed inside. What about you?
5. come

**Marta:** I _____ home from work when the rain started.
6. drive

I _____ to the radio, so I didn't hear the announcements. I couldn't see
7. not / listen

very well, so I pulled over by the side of the road. Some people _____
8. drive

still _____! I think the power went out because the traffic lights

_____. Most people _____ careful, but there were
9. not / work            10. be

accidents everywhere. I was so glad to get home safely.

**Talia:** Wow. No kidding.

## PRESENT PERFECT: INDEFINITE PAST

**Look at the chart. Compare the work experience of Mr. Birand and Ms. Cruz. Answer each question with a short answer. Then answer with a complete sentence using the present perfect.**

| Work Experience | Mr. Birand | Ms. Cruz |
|---|---|---|
| late shift | yes | no |
| weekend work | no | yes |
| work with computers | no | yes |
| hospital work | yes | yes |
| managed people | no | no |

**1.** Has Mr. Birand ever worked on weekends?

  _No, he hasn't. Mr. Birand has never worked on weekends._

**2.** Have Mr. Birand and Ms. Cruz ever worked in a hospital?

  _____

**3.** Has Mr. Birand ever worked with computers?

  _____

**4.** Has Ms. Cruz ever worked the late shift?

  _____

**5.** Have Mr. Birand and Ms. Cruz ever worked as a manager?

  _____

## PRESENT PERFECT WITH *FOR* AND *SINCE*

**Complete Sang Ho's conversation with a new coworker. Use *for*, *since*, or the present perfect form of the verbs.**

**Sang Ho:** Welcome to our department. How do you like it here so far?

**Julian:** Oh, I like it. I'm still getting used to being in Houston, though.

**Sang Ho:** Really? How long _____have_____ you _____been living_____ here?
1. live

**Julian:** Just _____ last month. So I _____ time to meet many people yet.
2.  3. not / have

**Sang Ho:** Well, there are a lot of great people here. I can introduce you to everyone.

**Julian:** Thanks. I'd like that! _____ you _____ here for a long time?
4. work

**Sang Ho:** Yeah, I _____ here _____ about five years. I really enjoy it.
5. work  6.

**Julian:** And _____ you always _____ in Houston?
7. be

**Sang Ho:** Well, I wasn't born here, but I _____ here _____ most of my life.
8. live  9.
It's a great city.

## GERUNDS AND INFINITIVES

**Look at the diagram. Then complete the paragraph about Paul's and Isabel's exercise habits. Use the infinitive or gerund form of the verbs in the diagram. More than one answer may be possible.**

| **Paul** | **Both** | **Isabel** |
| lift weights | walk | swim |
| play basketball | | ride her bike |

Paul and Isabel want to start a new exercise program. They both enjoy
(1.) _____*walking*_____, so they'll go to the park together every day to do that.
Paul also likes (2.) _____, so he will start a weight class at the gym.
Isabel will go with him to the gym. She can't stand (3.) _____, but
the gym has a great pool, and she loves (4.) _____. She also wants
(5.) _____ more often, perhaps to her job every day. Paul likes team
sports, so he might start (6.) _____ with some friends.

## GERUNDS AFTER PREPOSITIONS

**Complete the email. Add the correct preposition and use the gerund form of the verb.**

Hi Alan,

Thanks _____*for writing*_____. I apologize _____ your email sooner.
       1. write           2. not / answer
This week was really busy for me.

  I can't believe you bought a house. Congratulations! I bet you are excited
_____ to a new town. I wish we could afford to do that. Seth and
    3. move
I are tired _____ an apartment in the city. I doubt we'll be able to
      4. rent
buy a home any time soon. We're just not good _____ money.
                    5. save
Let's plan _____ together soon. I was thinking _____
     6. get               7. visit
you next weekend, if you are free. I'm looking forward _____ all
                           8. hear
about your new place.

Best wishes,

Linda

## MAKING REQUESTS

**Complete the conversation between a restaurant manager and a worker. Write an appropriate request with the words, or give an appropriate response. More than one answer may be possible.**

**Manager:** Jim, hi. I need to change the time for the meeting tomorrow. _____Can you help_____?
1. Can / help

**Jim:** _____Sure_____. What do you need me to do?
2.

**Manager:** First, _____ when the meeting room is available? We need it for one hour.
3. could / find out

**Jim:** _____. I'll check your agenda, too, and make sure the time is good for you.
4.

**Manager:** Perfect. Then, _____ all the participants to let them know the new time?
5. can / email

**Jim:** _____, I can do that. But I don't think I have the final list of participants.
6.

_____ it to me?
7. Would you mind / send

**Manager:** _____. I'll send it now. And thanks. I appreciate it.
8.

## INDIRECT OBJECTS

**Lara is writing an email to a friend about her weekend plans. Look at Lara's to-do list. Then complete the email. Use the verbs and a pronoun indirect object.**

| My To-Do List: | |
| --- | --- |
| ~~send card to Maya~~ | buy tie for Carlos |
| bring flowers to Mom | bake cake for Carlos |
| bring some magazines for Mom | lend my pasta maker to Karla |

Hi Gabi,

I'd love to visit you tomorrow, but I'm too busy! In the morning, I have to do errands. First, I need to go to the post office. My coworker Maya had a baby, and I want to (1.) _send her a card_. Then I need to pick up some things for my mom. She's in the hospital right now, so I'm going to (2.) _____, and I also want to (3.) _____. She gets really bored when she doesn't have anything to read. In the afternoon, my brother Carlos is having a birthday party. I'm going to (4.) _____. What do you think? Is that a good gift? I'm also going to (5.) _____. In the evening, I'm going to my friend Karla's house for dinner. I promised I'd (6.) _____.
Lara

## ADVERB CLAUSES OF TIME

**Read the instructions for using a washing machine. Then complete the sentences with the adverb clauses of time in parentheses.**

```
┌─────────────── Washing Machine Instructions ───────────────┐
│  • Make sure the machine is empty.                          │
│  • Load the clothes. Be sure to check the pockets of clothing and
│    remove any loose objects such as coins and pens.         │
│  • Select a temperature setting.                            │
│  • Add the soap to the soap drawer. Do not fill above the "max" line!
│  • Put coins in the coin slot. The START button will light up.
│  • Push the START button, and the WASH cycle will begin.    │
│  • Do not open the door of the washer while the machine is in use.
│  • The machine will shut off in 28 minutes.                 │
│  • Remove your clothing promptly so others may use the machine.
└─────────────────────────────────────────────────────────────┘
```

1. (before) _Before you use the washing machine_, make sure it is empty.

2. (as) _____ into the machine, check pockets for coins and other loose items.

3. (when) _____ to the soap drawer, make sure it doesn't go above the "max" line.

4. (before) _____ the START button, you need to put your money in the coin slot.

5. (after) _____, the START button lights up.

6. (after) _____, remove your clothing from the machine.

## PRESENT PERFECT WITH *ALREADY* AND *YET*

**Complete the conversation between a manager and an employee at a deli.
Use the present perfect form of the verbs in parentheses.**

**Manager:** Morning, Gary. How is the breakfast shift going?

**Gary:** Good. I (1. already / put) _have already put_ the breakfast rolls in the oven.

And of course, I (2. start) _____ the coffee machine.

**Manager:** Great. What about fruit?

**Gary:** Well, we (3. already / receive) _____ the morning delivery. But I

(4. not / set out) _____ the fruit in baskets yet. I was about to do that.

**Manager:** OK. (5. come in) _____ any phone orders _____ yet?

**Gary:** No, not yet. But we should start getting some soon.

**Manager:** All right. While you're waiting, you can make sure the trays are ready for customers.

**Gary:** Oh, I (6. already / do) _____ that. But I can start making up some sandwiches.

**Manager:** Good idea. Thanks.

## PRESENT PERFECT CONTINUOUS

**Complete the message with the correct present perfect continuous form of the verbs.**

Hey Tom,

I haven't seen you for a while. What (1. do) _have_ you _been doing_ lately? Are you still playing soccer on Saturdays? Things are going well for me. I (2. work) _____ very hard. You know me—I like to keep busy. It's great because I (3. save) _____ a lot of money since I (4. put) _____ in so much overtime. But I haven't had much time for anything else. That's why I (5. not / show up) _____ for soccer. But I miss it! I (6. spend) _____ some time with Elena recently. Do you remember her? She moved to Dallas to go to school, but she's back now. She (7. look) _____ for a job as an office assistant. I (8. try) _____ to help her with that. If you hear of anything, let me know! I have to run, but let's get together soon!

Charlie

## POSSESSIVE PRONOUNS

**Look at the picture. Then complete the conversation with the correct possessive pronouns.**

**Berta:** What a great party! I wish we didn't have to leave so soon.

**Marco:** I know. It was fun. Hey, are these your keys?

**Berta:** No, but I'll ask Oskar. They look like (1.) ____*his*____.

**Marco:** Can I get you your coat?

**Berta:** Thanks.

**Marco:** Is this one (2.) _____.

**Berta:** No. The blue one is (3.) _____.

**Marco:** Here you go. And is this your purse?

**Berta:** Yes, that's (4.) _____.

**Marco:** I can't find my gloves. They must be here somewhere.

**Berta:** Here's a pair. Are these (5.) _____?

**Marco:** Yes. Thanks! Oh, and these boots look like Anita's.

**Berta:** Yes, these are (6.) _____. Well, I guess we're all set to go.

**Marco:** Actually, I think we're still missing a couple of things.

**Berta:** Right—Anita and Oskar!

### PRESENT REAL CONDITIONAL

**Think about your vacation habits. On a separate piece of paper, write present real conditional sentences. Use the words from the word box and your own ideas.**

| | | | |
|---|---|---|---|
| go to the mountains | visit a big city | need to relax | travel with children |
| go to the beach | need to save money | want some excitement | |

> If I go to the mountains, I go skiing.

### COMPARATIVES

**Look at the ad. Then read the conversation. On a separate piece of paper, write 8 sentences to compare the two cameras. Use the comparative form of the adjectives from the word box.**

> cheap   clear   expensive   fast   good   heavy   slow   small

> The Nycam camera is faster than the Camcon camera.

**Clerk:** Can I help you with anything?

**Darla:** Yes, thanks. I want to buy my father a camera. I can't decide between the Camcon and the Nycam.

**Clerk:** OK. Let me ask you a question: What's your father going to use the camera for?

**Darla:** Well . . . he's an outdoorsman, so he likes taking pictures of animals and birds—stuff like that.

**Clerk:** I see. In that case, the Nycam might be a good choice. It has a fast shutter speed. The Camcon is a little slow. Unless your father photographs only turtles, camera speed is important!

**Darla:** True. Do both cameras have a zoom lens?

**Clerk:** Yes, they do. The Nycam zoom lens is really good. The photos are really clear, even if you are far away. The Camcon zoom lens is good, but not great. The photos aren't very clear.

**Darla:** The Nycam is really large. Will it be too heavy to carry around in the woods?

**Clerk:** Maybe. The Nycam is a full-size camera. It's a bit heavy. The Camcon is very light. It weighs just eight ounces and can fit in your pocket.

**Darla:** That's great. And the Camcon is half the price of the Nycam.

**Clerk:** True. The Camcon is really cheap. The Nycam is more expensive.

**Carla:** Hmm. You know, I still can't decide. I guess I need to think about it some more.

**Clerk:** No problem. But our sale on cameras ends this Friday, so don't wait too long!

**Camera Sale This Week!**

CamCon SlimLine
Original Price: $125
Sale Price: $99

Nycam CT200X
Original Price: $250
Sale Price: $199

## FUTURE REAL CONDITIONALS

On a separate piece of paper, write sentences using words from the word box and the future real conditional.

| | | |
|---|---|---|
| not eat junk food | shop for food when you are hungry | speak more English |
| exercise more often | use your cell phone while driving | catch a cold |
| take good care of your car | save a little money | |

*If you don't eat junk food, you will lose weight.*

## SUPERLATIVES

Complete the sentences about some incredible places and events.
Use the superlative form of the adjectives from the box.

| bad | busy | cold | deep | expensive | high | ~~old~~ | small |
|---|---|---|---|---|---|---|---|

1. A car made from a children's toy is ___*the smallest*___ car that can legally be driven on a road. It is only 41 inches (104.14 cm) high and 26 inches (66.04 cm) wide.

2. _____ mountain in the world is Mount Everest, in Nepal. It is 8,850 meters (29,035 feet) high.

3. One of _____ natural disasters in U.S. history was the San Francisco earthquake of 1906. It killed more than 3,000 people and destroyed over 80% of the city.

**"Wind Up" car**

**Shinjuku Station in Tokyo, Japan**

4. Which train station is _____ in the world? Shinjuku Station in Tokyo, Japan. An average of 3.64 million passengers use the station every day.

5. The Mariana Trench in the western Pacific Ocean is _____ part of the world's oceans. Parts of it are 11.03 kilometers (6.85 miles) deep.

6. Damascus, Syria, is one of _____ cities in the world. It was first settled at least 11,000 years ago.

7. _____ human-made object is the International Space Station. Its final cost will be over $100 billion.

8. _____ city is Verkhoyansk, Russia. The average temperature in January is –50.4 degrees Fahrenheit (–45.8° C).

**International Space Station**

# GRAMMAR REFERENCES

UNIT 1, LESSON 2, PAGE 7

**Review: Simple Present**

| Affirmative Statements | | |
|---|---|---|
| I<br>You<br>We<br>They | **take** | the bus to work. |
| He<br>She<br>Carla | **takes** | the train to work. |

| Negative Statements | | |
|---|---|---|
| I<br>You<br>We<br>They | **don't** | **drive**. |
| He<br>She<br>Carla | **doesn't** | **walk**. |

| Yes/No Questions | | |
|---|---|---|
| **Do** | you<br>they | **take** the train? |
| **Does** | he<br>she | **ride** a bike? |

| Short Answers | | | | | |
|---|---|---|---|---|---|
| Yes, | I<br>we<br>they | **do**. | No, | I<br>we<br>they | **don't**. |
| Yes, | he<br>she | **does**. | No, | he<br>she | **doesn't**. |

UNIT 1, LESSON 5, PAGE 11

| Common Quantifiers | | |
|---|---|---|
| **Quantity Expression** | **Used with Count Nouns** | **Used with Noncount Nouns** |
| any* (of the)<br>each (of the)<br>every<br>one (of the) | **Any** teacher can help you.<br>**Each** student has a book.<br>**Every** student has a desk.<br>**One** student is late. | No |
| both (of the)<br>a couple of<br>a few (of the)<br>many (of the)<br>several (of the)<br>two, three, etc. (of the) | **Both** students are late.<br>**A couple of** students need help.<br>**A few** students need books.<br>**Many** students attend class.<br>**Several** students need books.<br>**Two** students are in class early. | No |
| a little (of the)<br>much (of the) | No | They need **a little** help.<br>We don't have **much** time. |
| all (of the)<br>a lot of<br>lots of<br>most (of the)<br>none of the/no<br>some (of the) | **All** students must buy books<br>**A lot of** books are missing.<br>**Lots of** books are missing.<br>**Most** students are here today.<br>**None of** the students came late.<br>**Some of** the students came late. | **All** homework is due today.<br>They spent **a lot of** money.<br>They spent **lots of** money.<br>**Most** homework is useful.<br>I have **no** time today.<br>I need **some** time to finish. |

*Note: Use *any* with questions and negative statements for count and noncount.
 For example: Do you have **any** classes today? No, I don't have **any** classes today.
 Do you have **any** information about that? No, I don't have **any** information about that.

## UNIT 2, LESSON 2, PAGE 21

### Review: Future Forms

**Be going to: Statements**

| I | am | |
|---|---|---|
| You We They | are | (not) **going to take** the bus. |
| He She | is | |

**Be going to: Questions**

| | you | |
|---|---|---|
| **Are** | we they | **going to be** late? |
| **Is** | he she | |
| **When** are | you | **going to get** here? |
| **When** is | he | |

**Short Answers**

| | I | **am.** | | I'm not. |
|---|---|---|---|---|
| **Yes,** | we they | **are.** | **No,** | we're not. they're not. |
| | he she | **is.** | | he's not. she's not. |
| At 8:00. | | | | |

**Will: Statements**

| I You He She We They | **will** | **help** this weekend. | I You He She We They | **won't** | **come** on Friday. |
|---|---|---|---|---|---|

**Will: Questions**

| **Will** | you he she we they | **be** here tomorrow? | Yes, | I he she we they | **will.** | No, | I he she we they | **won't.** |
|---|---|---|---|---|---|---|---|---|
| **When** | **will** | you he they | **come**? | On Wednesday. At 2:00. | | | | |

## UNIT 3, LESSON 2, PAGE 35

**Review: Simple Past**

**Statements**

| I<br>You<br>He<br>She<br>We<br>They | **waited** | at the hospital. | I<br>You<br>He<br>She<br>We<br>They | **didn't wait** | for long. |
|---|---|---|---|---|---|

**Questions**

| **Did** | you<br>he<br>she<br>they | **talk** to the doctor? | **Yes,** | I<br>he<br>she<br>they | **did.** | **No,** | I<br>he<br>she<br>they | **didn't.** |
|---|---|---|---|---|---|---|---|---|
| How<br>long | **did** | you<br>he<br>they | **stay** there? | About two hours. | | | | |

# GRAMMAR REFERENCES

UNIT 3, LESSON 5, PAGE 39

## *Be:* Past Forms

| I<br>He<br>She | was/wasn't | in the hospital. |
|---|---|---|
| You<br>We<br>They | were/weren't | |

## Spelling Rules for Continuous Forms

For verbs ending in two consonants, add *-ing*. For example:

walk ⟶ walk**ing**

For verbs ending in two vowels + one consonant, add *-ing*. For example:

hear ⟶ hear**ing**

For verbs ending in *-e*, drop the *-e* and add *-ing*. For example:

smile ⟶ smil**ing**

telephone ⟶ telephon**ing**

For one-syllable verbs ending in one vowel + one consonant, double the consonant and add *-ing*. For example:

stop ⟶ stop**ping**

win ⟶ win**ning**

For two-syllable verbs ending in one vowel + one consonant, there are two rules:

**1.** If the first syllable is stressed, do not double the consonant. For example:

listen ⟶ listen**ing**

**2.** If the second syllable is stressed, double the consonant. For example:

prefer ⟶ prefer**ring**

For verbs ending in a consonant + *-y*, keep the *-y* and add *-ing*. For example:

study ⟶ study**ing**

play ⟶ play**ing**

For verbs ending in *-ie*, change the *-ie* to *-y* and add *-ing*. For example:

die ⟶ d**ying**

tie ⟶ t**ying**

# GRAMMAR REFERENCES

UNIT 4, LESSON 2, PAGE 49

## Common Irregular Verbs: Past Participles

| Base Form | Past | Past Participle | Base Form | Past | Past Participle |
|---|---|---|---|---|---|
| be | was, were | **been** | make | made | **made** |
| become | became | **become** | meet | met | **met** |
| begin | began | **begun** | pay | paid | **paid** |
| bring | brought | **brought** | put | put | **put** |
| buy | bought | **bought** | quit | quit | **quit** |
| catch | caught | **caught** | read | read | **read** |
| choose | chose | **chosen** | ride | rode | **ridden** |
| come | came | **come** | run | ran | **run** |
| cut | cut | **cut** | say | said | **said** |
| do | did | **done** | see | saw | **seen** |
| drink | drank | **drunk** | sell | sold | **sold** |
| drive | drove | **driven** | send | sent | **sent** |
| eat | ate | **eaten** | sit | sat | **sat** |
| feel | felt | **felt** | sleep | slept | **slept** |
| find | found | **found** | speak | spoke | **spoken** |
| fly | flew | **flown** | spend | spent | **spent** |
| get | got | **gotten** | stand | stood | **stood** |
| give | gave | **given** | steal | stole | **stolen** |
| go | went | **gone** | swim | swam | **swum** |
| grow | grew | **grown** | take | took | **taken** |
| have | had | **had** | teach | taught | **taught** |
| hear | heard | **heard** | tell | told | **told** |
| hold | held | **held** | think | thought | **thought** |
| hurt | hurt | **hurt** | try | tried | **tried** |
| keep | kept | **kept** | understand | understood | **understood** |
| know | knew | **known** | wake | woke (waked) | **woken (waked)** |
| leave | left | **left** | wear | wore | **worn** |
| let | let | **let** | win | won | **won** |
| lose | lost | **lost** | write | wrote | **written** |

# GRAMMAR REFERENCES

UNIT 5, LESSON 2, PAGE 63

## Verbs Followed by Gerunds

| | | |
|---|---|---|
| admit | don't mind | miss |
| appreciate | enjoy | practice |
| avoid | explain | quit |
| can't help | feel like | recommend |
| complete | finish | regret |
| consider | give up (stop) | risk |
| discuss | keep (on) | suggest |
| dislike | mind | |

## Verbs Followed by Infinitives

| | | |
|---|---|---|
| agree | expect | prepare |
| appear | fail | pretend |
| arrange | hope | promise |
| ask | learn | refuse |
| can't afford | manage | seem |
| choose | mean | volunteer |
| decide | need | want |
| demand | offer | wish |
| deserve | plan | would like |

## Verbs Followed by Gerunds or Infinitives

| | | |
|---|---|---|
| begin | hate | remember |
| can't stand | like | start |
| continue | love | stop |
| forget | prefer | try |

UNIT 6, LESSON 5, PAGE 81

## Review: Object Pronouns

| Subject Pronoun | Object Pronoun | Example Sentence |
|---|---|---|
| I | **me** | I need the report. Please give it to **me**. |
| you | **you** | You have the files. Linda sent them to **you**. |
| he | **him** | He knows her address. Ask **him**. |
| she | **her** | Mrs. Brown needs directions. Please help **her**. |
| we | **us** | We have a question. Can you help **us**? |
| they | **them** | The nurses can help. Ask **them** your questions. |

# GRAMMAR REFERENCES

## UNIT 9, LESSON 5, PAGE 123

### Spelling Rules for Comparative Adjectives

For most adjectives with one syllable, add -er. For example:
cheap ⟶ cheap**er**

For adjectives ending in -y, change the -y to -i and add -er. For example:
easy ⟶ eas**ier**

For adjectives ending in -e, add -r. For example:
safe ⟶ safe**r**

For adjectives ending in one consonant + one vowel + one consonant, double the second consonant and add -er. For example:
thin ⟶ thinn**er**

For adjectives with two or more syllables, add *more* or *less* before the adjective. For example:
expensive ⟶ **more** expensive
**less** expensive

## UNIT 10, LESSON 5, PAGE 137

### Spelling Rules for Superlative Adjectives

For most adjectives with one syllable, add -est. For example:
cheap ⟶ cheap**est**

For adjectives ending in -y, change the -y to -i and add -est. For example:
easy ⟶ eas**iest**

For adjectives ending in -e, add -st. For example:
safe ⟶ safe**st**

For adjectives ending in one consonant + one vowel + one consonant, double the second consonant and add -est. For example:
thin ⟶ thin**nest**

For adjectives with two or more syllables, add *most* or *least* before the adjective: For example:
expensive ⟶ **most** expensive
**least** expensive

# WORD LIST

## UNIT 1

**Lesson 1**
be into something
be supposed to
for once
gorgeous
heavy

**Lesson 3**
concentrate
likely
nutrition
protein
research
skip
startling

**Lesson 4**
a ceiling
cover a possession
leak
permission
renter's insurance
rounds

**Lesson 7**
an active ingredient
an allergic reaction
a capsule
discard
a dosage
drowsiness

an expiration date
a milligram
a rash
a tablet

**Lesson 8**
all set
borrow
dead
a favor
lend
work out

**Lesson 9**
benefits
commute
full-time
an hourly wage
insurance
on-the-job training
part-time
a retirement plan

## UNIT 2

**Lesson 1**
break down
construction
cover for someone
a detour
icy
make up time
take notes
a traffic accident

**Lesson 3**
chronic
an excuse

fire someone
a GPS
an impression
odd
snooze
sympathetic
a traffic jam

**Lesson 4**
catch up
a database
enter data
an icon

owe someone
save
transfer a call

**Lesson 7**
a block
a cross-street
an intersection

**Lesson 9**
adapt
assess
an attitude
criticism

economy
efficiently
minimum
multi-task
negotiate
specific
tough

# WORD LIST

## UNIT 3

**Lesson 1**
back then
calm
a car seat
expecting a baby
a lap
a nervous wreck

**Lesson 3**
appropriate
avoid
examine
grip
a handle
an injury

prevent
a risk
squat
tuck in
twist

**Lesson 4**
apologetic
an appetite
build up
an intern
keep someone company
a regulation
run into someone
upset

**Lesson 6**
a campaign
common sense
distracted
fake
a fine
hilarious
humorous
a manhole
a pedestrian
a sewer
stroll

**Lesson 8**
a bandage
bother
catch
every other day
go over information
stretch

**Lesson 9**
accredited
administer
a license
monitor
status

## UNIT 4

**Lesson 1**
an ER
fast-paced
job satisfaction
an OR
rewarding
stressful
a transfer

**Lesson 3**
culinary
enlist
evaluate

flap
mouthwash
a movie studio
a scuba diver
simulate
a submarine

**Lesson 4**
elderly
envy
exhausting
intense
an opportunity

outpatient
a regret

**Lesson 6**
a 401K plan
base rate
a deduction
FICA
gross pay
HR
income tax
Medicare
net pay

overtime
Social Security
a wage
year-to-date

**Lesson 8**
due somewhere
original
take on a task
workaholic

# WORD LIST

## UNIT 5

**Lesson 1**
do aerobics
go jogging
lift weights

**Lesson 4**
blame
impress
incompetent
insist
officially
praise
tricky
work under someone

**Lesson 6**
a burden
handle something
negative
objective
prevent
realize
shirk
a slacker
a whiner

**Lesson 7**
an alarm system
an amenity
carpeting
a complex

an eat-in kitchen
a half bath
off-street parking
a square foot
storage
utilities
a walk-up

**Lesson 8**
a balcony
a full bath
a laundromat
a patio
a walk-in closet

**Lesson 9**
military service
self-employment

## UNIT 6

**Lesson 1**
a binder
a file
file a document
look something up
a participant
prioritize
a priority
restock
scan a document
a supply room

**Lesson 3**
alcoholism
cancer
currently
depression
diabetes
high blood pressure
insomnia
a migraine
osteoporosis
penicillin
tuberculosis

**Lesson 4**
an agenda
be unavailable
an inbox
just in case
reach someone

**Lesson 6**
a concern
frankly
a health care provider
an illness

a side effect
a symptom
a treatment option

**Lesson 8**
a consultation
fIll out
an opening
paperwork
reschedule

# WORD LIST

## UNIT 7

**Lesson 1**
come up
a diet card
double-check
fall into place
load
preparation
treat
a wing

**Lesson 3**
a coach
confidence

convince
encourage
juggle
a letter of reference
literacy
social services
volunteer
a volunteer

**Lesson 4**
about to do something
capable
clear

enthusiastic
run low on something
a staff
stock
value

**Lesson 8**
a degree
a favor
graduation
proud
whichever

**Lesson 9**
incentive
mentor
a reimbursement

## UNIT 8

**Lesson 1**
commendable
demanding
empathy
an evaluation
improvement
maintain
overall
a performance
rapport

**Lesson 4**
belongings
digital
an effort
missing
out of sight
a style
taste

**Lesson 6**
APR
a balance

a consumer
a credit limit
debt
a mortgage
no-fee
outstanding

**Lesson 7**
attracted to something
a charity
a donation
expire

fine print
an offer
terms

**Lesson 8**
blow off steam
a club
downtown
unwind
wind down

# WORD LIST

## UNIT 9

**Lesson 1**
a bargain
a blog
clog up
a coupon
a deal
a discount
junk mail
savvy
subscribe

**Lesson 3**
a circular
essential
floral

locate
pleasant
resist
a sensation
a trick

**Lesson 4**
convenient
a crowd
an IT department
obviously
a pain
related
return a purchase
the Stone Ages

tech-savvy
a whiz

**Lesson 6**
a brick-and-mortar store
an exception
merchandise
packaging
a policy
a store credit

**Lesson 8**
a barbecue
a bunch of
a cook-off

a grill
Memorial Day
observe a holiday
a picnic

**Lesson 9**
awkward
a disability
ethnicity
gender
illegal
marital status
recognize

## UNIT 10

**Lesson 1**
advance
afford
oversee
a path
a promotion
report to someone
tuition

**Lesson 3**
an academic advisor
analyze
a credit
interpret

a lecture
a prerequisite
a procedure
a proposal
statistics
a theory
a thesis

**Lesson 4**
admire
capable
considerate
diagnose
enthusiastic

judgment
keep one's cool
patient
pressure
a resident

**Lesson 7**
an argument
a dropout
an expert
an investment
justify
a network
think critically

**Lesson 8**
boost
explore
open up
a possibility
solid
talk something over

**Lesson 9**
documentation
an orientation